Improving Schools

Improving Schools

Simple Approaches and Understandings to Realize Growth

Kevin Popadines

ROWMAN & LITTLEFIELD
Lanham • Boulder • New York • London

Published by Rowman & Littlefield
An imprint of The Rowman & Littlefield Publishing Group, Inc.
4501 Forbes Boulevard, Suite 200, Lanham, Maryland 20706
www.rowman.com

86-90 Paul Street, London EC2A 4NE, United Kingdom

Copyright © 2024 by Kevin Popadines

All rights reserved. No part of this book may be reproduced in any form or by any electronic or mechanical means, including information storage and retrieval systems, without written permission from the publisher, except by a reviewer who may quote passages in a review.

British Library Cataloguing in Publication Information Available

Library of Congress Cataloging-in-Publication Data

Names: Popadines, Kevin, 1978– author.
Title: Improving schools : simple approaches and understandings to realize growth / Kevin Popadines.
Description: Lanham, Maryland : Rowman & Littlefield, 2024. | Includes bibliographical references. | Summary: "This text is an exploration of school and educational improvement. It explores areas of focus that can immediately be added to improvement plans and daily practice"— Provided by publisher.
Identifiers: LCCN 2023044842 (print) | LCCN 2023044843 (ebook) | ISBN 9781475865264 (cloth) | ISBN 9781475865271 (paperback) | ISBN 9781475865288 (epub)
Subjects: LCSH: School improvement programs—United States. | Teachers—Training of—United States. | Teachers—In service learning—United States. | Adult education—United States.
Classification: LCC LB2822.82 .P65 2024 (print) | LCC LB2822.82 (ebook) | DDC 371.2/07—dc23/eng/20231027
LC record available at https://lccn.loc.gov/2023044842
LC ebook record available at https://lccn.loc.gov/2023044843

Contents

Preface	vii
Acknowledgments	ix
Introduction	1
Chapter 1: Adult Learning Theory: A Missing Piece	11
Chapter 2: Adult Learning Experiences, Not So Fast	23
Chapter 3: Now We Are Ready for Learning Experiences	29
Chapter 4: Human Resource Development	35
Chapter 5: Local Resources	47
Chapter 6: Licensure and Assessment: A Path Forward	57
Chapter 7: Technology and Online Learning: The Shrinking Educational Universe	65
Chapter 8: Climate: A Broad and Vital Area of Focus	73
Chapter 9: The Educator	81
Chapter 10: Putting It All Together	89
Bibliography	99
About the Author	101

Preface

Having over twenty years of experience in education, with roles spanning from the classroom to the basketball court, golf course to the district level across different states, organizations, and countries, I have seen opportunities missed and cycles of stagnation repeated with little effort to learn from those mistakes. Please do not misunderstand, I have worked for great leaders, schools, districts, and organizations. While there was a lot to celebrate and a lot to admire, there could and should have been more.

This does not mean that those who could affect change were unable to or refused do the right thing. I saw great practices and initiatives in place and executed. However, I also saw missed opportunities, failures to meet all students' needs, and room for growth. Where does this not exist? I have yet to see a model or exemplary school, let alone a model district or organization. I hope to one day do so, but until then, shouldn't everyone's focus be on improving what we have? Change is a complicated concept. If too much change within a school or institution is attempted, nothing gets done correctly or well.

One of the most powerful tools we have in education is reflection. Looking back at my own practice in the classroom or as a coach, there was so much I wish I could and would have done differently. My approach would have been more student centered. I would have trusted best practices to bring more inquiry to my students and would have used more data to plan more powerful, differentiated lessons. I would have been more in tune with my students and been a bigger advocate for them and their needs. There is always room to grow and get better.

As someone who designs and delivers professional learning for adult learners, my responsibility is to be a reflective practitioner. My job is to meet adult learners' needs and, despite being hired for multiple jobs in this field, I did much of my own learning and research on how to meet adult learners' needs. Again, looking back at my work over the years, there is much I wish I could have done differently.

This text was born out of reflection, experience, and a variety of roles. Looking back at all the places I have been fortunate enough to work and be a part of their educational community, I see no fault and failure, but I see opportunity. Education is a demanding field that pushes those involved to their limits. Time is a precious asset that is in demand. So, it is understandable that reflection is not the first place that time is spent. Couple that with the idea that improvement is often anchored around a strategy or a small data point, and opportunities continue to present themselves for different educational approaches to yield improvement.

Obviously, if there was a quick fix for our nation's schools, a full book would not be needed. We all know that a quick fix does not exist. However, there are areas that have not been focused on enough or with the correct lens. The goal of this text is to give readers a perspective on areas that could provide, given the right ability to affect change, a chance to improve one's school. All students deserve the best educational experience, and continually improving a school is the simplest path to get there.

This text is not meant to be an exhaustive research digest. While there is some research and some citations, it is meant to focus more on the application from a practitioner's view. The hope, and ultimate goal, for writing this book is to give those in a position of influence some ideas they can apply in order to achieve that elusive goal of school improvement. I hope that leaders find ways to leverage some of the ideas present in this text and can move the needle in their school, district, or institution.

Acknowledgments

We are all the product of our environment. We are also a reflection of those who have been a part of that environment. There are so many people who helped me get to a situation where I can attempt to affect change in education. I have been blessed working for and learning from dynamic leaders. Whether they have realized it or not, my practice of watching and learning from leaders is a never-ending process. Every new leader I encounter provides an opportunity for me to learn and grow. While I would love to list each by name, I know that this would lead to leaving someone important out. However, please know that I am thankful for all the tutelage and knowledge that has been shared with me along the way by those who I have worked for and with. The diverse strengths, approaches, and visions that each person has possessed has served as a wonderful opportunity for me to reflect, apply, and grow.

There is, however, a brief list of people I would like to personally acknowledge. My father taught me the value of education, hard work, and, most importantly, believing in myself. He raised me with high expectations and love while teaching me that if I wanted something, I would have to work hard for it. Those important lessons were not lost on me, at least not always. I never stopped trying to continue my education and add to my credentials. I never stopped seeing what opportunities were out there. I never stopped trying to impact the world of education because of my father's lessons. Thank you for putting me on a pathway to what I deem as a successful career in education.

My mother, who is sadly not still with us and will not see this book in print, gave me more than a son could ask for. My mother was the kindest person I have known. She tried to instill that in me, and this was a big part of what led to my path to the field of education and helping others. She was also my biggest advocate. Some people say they are proud of someone and may mean it, but my mother, when she said she was proud of me, everyone knew that she meant it. Any accomplishment in my life, whether small and trivial or a milestone, was shared by my mother with anyone who would listen. Before

I was reflective enough to see this as the love for a child that only some special parents can have, I was sometimes shy or embarrassed to see my mother speak of me as if I were a Nobel Prize winner when I accomplished something I that deemed as small or insignificant. Yet, as I got older, I started to wish that I should have appreciated every moment of that pride more than I had because those are special things. Her belief and pride in me helped to drive me more and show me that if I wanted to do something, that I would be able to do it, no matter how small or grand. I know my mother is smiling as I both type this and as others read it, and I hope she knows that her influence on me and love for me are appreciated more every day.

My wife Lauren and my daughter Isabella both make me a better person and give me a greater purpose. Lauren has been my rock and inspiration through countless degrees, job changes, moves, and life events. She has shown an unwavering belief in me, my goals, and dreams. Having a life partner who makes you a better person and gives you the courage to dream has been a blessing and an honor.

As a couple who lived together twenty years before having a daughter, much time was spent doing things that we wanted to do. We earned degrees together, traveled, and became best friends. Becoming a father after forty plus years of life changes one's ability to both find and have time to work on anything beyond being a part of the family and holding a primary job. However, my wife knows and understands that there is a lot that I want to accomplish, and the time I have already invested in my degrees is something I wanted to use to create something to benefit others and with which to push myself. Furthermore, I want to leave something behind that will survive long beyond my days. In doing this I strive to do things in life that will hopefully have my daughter be as proud of me as my mother was.

Finally, I would not have authored a book if not for the inspiration of my dissertation chair, mentor, and friend, Dr. Alan Wimberley. Alan never saw me as someone who had not arrived. He saw me as someone who had something to say and share with the world. He inspired me to leverage my degrees into a vehicle to share my voice. I hope this product is up to his standard.

I feel blessed to have so many influential people in my life and hope that this book lives up to each of their expectations.

Introduction

What does "improvement" mean? It is an ambiguous term. Improvement encompasses the idea of getting better or moving forward, but what does it really mean? Now think about the idea of improvement in terms of education. What does school improvement mean? If one were to ask 100 different educators, administrators, and school leaders this question, it would likely produce 100 different answers. Even if a collective understanding of the ideas of improvement and school improvement were achieved, is there ever an adequate target or end goal to get a single school—let alone the nation's education—where it could, should, or needs to be?

Take a moment to reflect about the state of education. Are schools in the United States performing as well as they could be? Are students receiving the best possible education each and every day? Is every stone left unturned to affect change in the world of education to match the change occurring in the world? The educational community cannot look in the mirror and pretend that there is not more work to be done regarding improvement. While pockets of excellence exist and need to be celebrated, there is always opportunity for improvement, and this text is designed and written to explore areas where improvement is both needed and attainable.

Teachers and principals do not take an oath like those within the medical field. However, those in education have some inherent responsibilities that sometimes require gentle reminders. There is a responsibility to center thinking around what is best for all students. There is a responsibility for continual growth and improvement. This is increasingly important because education is a dynamic field where theory, practice, and resources are continually changing. There exists a responsibility to be an invested part of the larger school community. This creates the responsibility of improving not just personally but systematically within each community. This text was written with those responsibilities in mind.

This text will explore small yet significant steps that individuals, schools, and organizations can explore and implement to improve education. Tearing down public and private educational systems is not a realistic option and not an option that needs to happen. As the world changes faster than ever, now is not the time to put a stop to educating this nation's youth; however, it is the time for honest evaluation and improvement. If this text does nothing more than to give someone in this noble field time and opportunity to reflect on focused areas, then those invested will be moving in the right direction. Hopefully, though, everyone will strive for more.

Please do not confuse this text with a call to vilify teachers and administrators. It is quite the opposite. The nation's schools are powerful institutions that are filled with caring, knowledgeable, and talented professionals. However, it is a responsibility within this or any field to want to make as much of a positive difference as possible. This text will hopefully give these professionals some innovative ideas on how to better affect positive change for students, schools, and districts so that the practices currently being done well can be done better, and areas of growth can soon become areas of success.

Let this be a call to action. Let this be a chance to step away from what has always been done. Let this be an opportunity to challenge the status quo. This text will examine approaches, theory, resources; how one tackles learning and development; and how to utilize them. This book is not exhaustive, as there is always more that can be done; however, it does look at different angles and aspects with most being related and a few that could be approached as discrete. Schools are like learners—no two are the same, and the path to improvement for each will be different, so read with a mindset to affect change given the influence of the reader.

Two of the primary areas of focus in this text will be teachers and administrators/principals. Research has found that teachers have the single greatest impact on a child's education compared to any other factor.[1] The Wallace Foundation concluded as the result of a two-decade study that replacing a below-average with an above-average principal in an elementary school would yield almost three months of math and reading gains for students each year in that school.[2] The impact of teachers and principals on the success of students and the school is undeniable and focusing considerable time and attention on them in improvement efforts is vital to seeing results.

This journey starts by looking at some of the root causes for why schools may not function as efficiently as they can. This will help to lay a foundation for where and how some change could and should occur. This begins with an idea that is often viewed as positive in the country but can be causing issues that may prevent some schools from flourishing. How diverse educators are and how they are a product of varied educational and professional experiences is overlooked. This author is not suggesting that anyone wants robotic teachers that are all the same; however, there needs to be exploration of the challenges that diverse backgrounds of teachers and staff present.

Diversity is a term that can mean many different things in different contexts. For the context of this text, diversity will encompass both educational backgrounds and work/field experiences one has in education. This applies to both educators and principals. This understanding is important to consider regarding how those differences have an impact on the outcomes of learning experiences provided for teachers and principals.

One of the things that helps this country have a wealth of educational options and opportunities is the idea of choice. After high school, educational options include trade schools; community, private, public, and for-profit colleges; and universities, all of which in different states have various strengths and offer many degree options. Looking at the field of education, students can take many paths toward a career. A traditional option may be a four-year degree; however, those degrees look different from one school to the next. Students have options in what courses they can take within a degree, and this yields experiential and knowledge differences in teachers.

One must also think about the alternate route, where someone with a non-education degree or a previous career can work toward a teaching license. This opportunity allows professionals to enter the field of education at a different point in their lives. This grants students access to teachers who bring experiences from fields where they previously worked. It also brings teachers into the profession with less coursework in educational learning theory and less prior field experience in the form of student teaching. Many successful teachers have taken this route; however, for the purpose of this line of thinking, this can cause a greater divide in skill and knowledge within staff.

Most states have different requirements for licensure and different paths to fill the many vacancies that occur in the education systems each year. The makeup of the nation's teachers possesses skills, degrees, experiences, and backgrounds so diverse that one could not begin to compare any two teachers fully and accurately. This gap is only compounded by the varying ages of educators and knowing that coursework has changed over time. Technology, theory, resources, and standards have also significantly changed throughout the past years and decades.

What could be the problem with many options in how to enter education? Furthermore, what could be the issue with having a rich and diverse set of educators? The short answer is, nothing, as the system has operated this way since its inception. Similarly: nothing, if one recognizes these differences and approaches of educators through a full understanding of the challenges that such a varied set of experiences present. There is a true strength in diversity that should provide a well-rounded staff and a wealth of experience. However, that strength is only powerful if recognized, leveraged, and differentiated for during learning opportunities.

With diversity comes strength. This is true if one embraces those differences in all situations. If those in education embrace this diversity, these strengths and any areas that need improvement for employees could be leveraged. One would know all the training and learning experiences they have taken part in. One would know what educational strategies they have been adequately trained in and mastered. One would know as much about teachers and staff as is known about students. While leaders will admit they do not know everyone well enough, do those who know them well use that information effectively when planning learning experiences?

This work should be approached through a lens of improvement and growth. Approaching improvement and growth requires honest and regular reflection and assessment. Do schools and systems differentiate their learning for adults with the same effort they differentiate learning for students? Do schools and systems make data-driven decisions to give adult learners experiences that meet them where they are, where their needs lie, when they are ready to learn, and are applied to problems they face in their lives? Does everyone in a position to teach adults even know how to approach designing learning experiences that meet the unique needs that adult learners possess?

Anyone currently in the field of education who has been employed for a little while and is not lucky enough to be in a top, exemplary situation has sat through the "standard" approach of professional learning that is a one-size-fits-all staff development. Everyone gathers in the school library or cafeteria and receives training on a predetermined topic while students have the day off and teachers scramble to get approval to schedule a medical appointment. An agenda is emailed to teachers and staff a few days ahead of time, if participants are lucky, with reminders of what to bring, where to go, and what they will be learning about.

Most in education have been there and continue to be there regularly. These occur whether the school is in a state that requires accreditation or simply has learning experiences linked to an action plan, school goal, or initiative. Broad approaches to training and learning experiences all too often mirror these less than effective events in schools and districts. If a teacher in a classroom were to ignore the differences in their learners and continually use a one-size-fits-all approach, two things would happen. Many students would fail to have their needs met and administration would take notice and frown on such poor practice.

So why is this tolerated when approaching learning for adults? Why is continuing down this path of ineffective learning experiences for people in such a critical profession still happening? There are many reasons. Any time there is something wrong in the setting of education, money is often identified as the problem, the solution, or both. It is more cost-effective to conduct in-house training by leveraging administrators, teacher leaders, and other free or less expensive sources. A school or district could hire an outside entity to design and deliver learning experiences to better meet more learners' needs, but this would come at the expense of something else.

Convenience is another reason. With professional development days inserted on a school calendar months before the start of a school year, it is convenient to conduct training for goals and initiatives while having an organized, predetermined plan for what teachers and staff can expect to see throughout the year. An arc of learning, or long-range pathway, may be created, allowing everything to have a level of transparency. For those providing, organizing, or helping plan the learning, there would exist a convenience factor. This could be likened to a teacher having all of their worksheets copied and ready to go for each day of the school year before day one.

As any good educator will attest, planning by using data, differentiating instruction, and other best practices is not easy and takes time. Imagine the time it would take to gather data on a one-hundred-person staff, make a personalized learning plan for each member, and have the facilitators available and ready to deliver learning as needed when needed. Of course, this sounds both difficult and unreasonable, but while it is difficult, is it unreasonable? Is meeting the individual needs of all young students unreasonable or unexpected? Then why is it different when considering learning for the adult learners who educate these same children?

Think about a typical elementary school teacher in the United States. The average class size in America for elementary schools is approximately twenty-two students. Each day an elementary school teacher is asked to create data-driven lessons in mathematics, English language arts, science, and social studies. This is a safe and low estimate as some schools require technology, health, and other subjects. If one looks at the core four classes, that is four times twenty-two or plans that account for eighty-eight learners. This is repeated daily. So, is good design asking too much, especially with the low frequency of staff development?

However, there is an underlying root cause that is often ignored, not by malice but by ignorance. One thing many of those diverse paths to becoming an educator have in common is something they regularly lack. Similarly, the budget-friendly, poorly-differentiated learning experiences also have the same deficiency. That common thread is an understanding of and ability to apply sound adult learning theory into the practice of educating teachers. Adult learning theory sometimes makes a brief appearance in an undergraduate theory course, or in some graduate level study. However, it is not a heavy focus, but it should be.

Administrators and teacher leaders are often tasked with designing and delivering learning experiences for learners who are adults. They apply what they are familiar with—pedagogy—causing an unintentional disconnect. It is not a stretch to say that schools could be better. It is not a stretch to say that training experiences within schools can be better. It is certainly not a stretch to say that one should always be looking to improve. There is no shame in making mistakes if one is willing to learn from them. However, has there been reflection, in education, regarding why there are not more successful learning experiences for teachers that intentionally apply adult learning theory?

There is a litany of reasons why schools are not reaching their full potential. Easy answers include varying length of school days, lack of resources, variance in home support, different standards, and different curricula, just to name a few. But if there was a magic bullet in those or other factors, it would have been tried already. There is always a call to hire more qualified teachers. Perhaps new hires help, but what about tenured staff that account for most of the workforce? One must think broadly and look not at replacing all teachers but maximizing and improving the knowledge and skills of the ones that are in place.

There is a reason adults and children do not thrive in the same educational settings. Adult and child learners are different on many levels. Adults and children have varying amounts of experiences and different goals, motivations, and needs. There is a lot that separates how someone in their fifties and someone who just turned ten years old can and should learn. With that being said and acknowledged, what is being done to ensure that these differences are being addressed when learning is designed and delivered?

Imagine being asked to do a job that one was not professionally trained to do. Tomorrow the task is driving 200 miles per hour around a track. One could be asked to complete the electrical wiring of a new house. Perhaps one will be asked to remove dangerous wildlife from someone's backyard. While these may seem extreme, doing a job that one is not trained to do is not a path for a successful experience. Yet experiences dealing with educating adults are often designed and facilitated by people not fully prepared nor equipped to have that role, let alone to be successful with it.

Who teaches our teachers? Principals are often tasked with producing and facilitating professional learning for teachers. Nothing in an educational leadership degree uniquely qualifies a principal to educate teachers. This practice was born out of necessity. Teachers are also tasked or volunteer to lead and design professional learning. These teachers may be department chairs, an improvement team member or teacher on special assignment, TOSA. Internal design and facilitation are leveraged to lead much of the learning that is provided for teachers. Unfortunately, a high number of those filling this necessary role lack a proper background in theory or experience with teaching adults.

Educating adults is not limited to the field of education. All industries face the need to have employees adapt, be educated, and grow. If businesses can improve and grow, then why are schools not all able to do the same thing? Part of the advantage that businesses have over schools is that businesses with human resource departments have people who have been trained to teach and work with adults and only adults. Those tasked with a similar charge in education have been primarily trained to instruct children. This is a problem that is and has been right in front of the education community but is unfortunately overlooked and ignored.

Education is the easy area to scrutinize as those working in it should have a high level of theory and practice in the designing of instruction. Yet most of that training and experience is working with children. Ask anyone who works in a high school how they would feel about teaching in an elementary school or vice versa. The majority of those polled would be hesitant. Teaching first grade math is quite different from teaching sophomore geometry. Yet, both scenarios fall under the umbrella of pedagogy. Adult learners do not fit that theory. Yet those often charged to work with adult learners in education were trained to apply pedagogy.

This book will look at much of what was discussed in this opening chapter in more depth. It will look at viable solutions to what is missing when it comes to designing and facilitating learning experiences for adult learners. This text will approach all ideas through a solutions-based approach. The goal in this text is to create opportunities to identify areas in need of improvement and offer some suggestions about how one can approach them. This text does not look to point fingers nor suggest that starting everything over from zero is the correct path forward.

This text will scratch the surface of adult learning theory, specifically andragogy, and how adults can best learn. This will lead to finding solutions to identified problems while beginning to create a roadmap for improvement. This will include looking at scale, capacity, and how to begin to move the needle, all the while understanding that this problem has a moving target. As technology, initiatives, and even students change, there is a need for flexibility with those targets and approaches. Schools look different today than they did a few years ago and college graduates each year come to the workforce with new skill sets. Recognizing this is a necessary and positive step.

This text will explore the responsibility of an adult to continue their education. Self-reflection and self-improvement need to be a part of any continual process. If one does not recognize this need within themself, how can one improve in a world with ever-changing students? This text will include exploring some typical licensure renewal processes that allow adults to choose learning for themselves while recognizing how this can further widen the gaps in knowledge between already diverse staffs. This will be followed with why looking at a systemic approach to learning experiences that adhere to best practices in adult learning can be a positive way forward.

This text will examine the roles of administrators and building principals. This will include taking a reflective look at what they are doing and what they need to be doing to realize the term instructional leader. This continues with examining how walking the walk and giving principals the opportunity to do what is really needed from their job can dynamically affect improvement efforts in schools. These ideas will be paired together with seeing schools through a lens of human resource development and what that can look like as well as how it can affect operations in a school.

A large focus of the content will be looking at how there exist resources that are not being maximized or not being utilized that can help improve schools. Many of these resources are at community and four-year colleges and universities. Identifying these resources and areas where they can impact improvement efforts is a positive early step. Collaboration and maximizing what is available are powerful methods to affect change and are areas where many schools and districts can grow to improve. Many of the ideas identified in this text are mutually beneficial to all parties.

This text will examine how the educational universe is shrinking. Online learning has opened the door for more adults to gain increased access to educational opportunities, skills, and knowledge. Online degrees are readily available on one's device. More importantly, when examining systematically improving schools and districts there are increased opportunities to access learning from anywhere with internet connectivity. Continuing education credits offer opportunities for common learning to occur or be created. Massive open online courses (MOOCs) and Edcamps can offer free opportunities for online learning to help educators learn and grow.

Time will be spent looking at the idea of climate. Climate will be explored from the traditional sense that includes looking at the physical attributes of a learning space. Climate will also be discussed from an adult learner perspective. This will center around how a trusting, respectful, and supportive atmosphere are key attributes of a more successful learning environment. Looking at climate as a means to tie together an adult learning approach, with a proper instructional leader role, along with properly leveraged local resources, and technology use will help create a road map for how to enact improvement at one's school or district.

Finally, time will be spent looking at the teacher. A teacher's health and well-being are vital for a functioning school. School improvement efforts that ignore the teacher, their satisfaction, and providing them with structures and support will be incomplete and will not be a sustainable initiative. In a time where the social and emotional needs of students are at the forefront of school resources and planning, educators need to be focused on with a similar level of urgency to help combat the rising attrition rates and lack of job satisfaction.

The areas that will be explored in this text—adult learning theory, human resource development, leveraging local resources, online learning, climate and supporting teachers—are not innovative ideas. Yet these are all areas that may be overlooked, taken for granted, and still have room to improve. Being a reflective practitioner and giving honest assessments of how one's school or district is functioning and how well students are benefiting from improvement systems in place are where one should start this process. The reader should approach all reading and learning through a solution-oriented mindset and determine what changes one can realistically help realize.

There are no quick-fix solutions to the problems those in education face and want to solve. However, starting the conversation, looking through fresh eyes, and being honest about where one is and where one wants to be is a positive early step. All schools have room to grow. Educators are the engines that can affect change. However, affecting the change of those engines is a difficult but necessary task. Better learning cannot take place in schools until growth-minded professionals find meaningful ways to improve practice and provide the experiences and support to do so.

Keep an open mind while continuing in this text. Think as a solution-oriented reader and learner. Picture a system where learning is approached to best meet the needs of each learner and where each learner is the willing and eager participant in self-improvement. Think of innovation and approaching weaknesses with refocused ideas and opportunities to overcome these challenges. While one may not reach a full blueprint to success immediately, one will hopefully affect enough change in thought and approach to take the important steps toward a new and more effective approach to improving classrooms, schools, and beyond.

NOTES

1. Opper, *Teachers Matter*, 1.
2. Grissom et al., "How Principals Affect Students and Schools: A Systemic Synthesis of Two Decades of Research," 13.

Chapter 1

Adult Learning Theory

A Missing Piece

The first place to start this journey toward improvement is by taking a look at if and how sound adult learning principles are being applied when teachers are receiving professional learning. Since teachers have the greatest impact on student success, continuing the education of educators with the best design and approaches possible should be a top priority. A teacher who refuses to apply sound pedagogy practices for their students would not have a long career education. Yet, intentional application of adult learning theory principles in learning designed for teachers, staff, and principals is often severely lacking.

Here is a brief exercise to establish if a recent learning event an adult participated in was designed with best practices for adult learners. Thinking about a recent experience, did learners know why they needed to know what was being taught? Did the learners have any self-direction in the learning experience? Were the unique experience levels of the participants effectively leveraged to aid in the learning process? Were learners at a place and time in their lives where they were ready to receive the learning? Did learners see this experience as something that would solve a real problem? Finally, were learners intrinsically motivated to participate?

It is by design that this text starts with an examination on which improvements need to be made based on how needs are not currently being met. The neuroscience of how one learns paints a dark picture of the damage that poor learning experiences can have on a learner. Powerful positive emotions experienced while learning will positively support long-term memory, while strong negative emotions will block long-term memory.[1] It has also been determined that stressful learning can activate the fight or flight response in learners.[2] Improvement requires learning that is intentionally designed for adult learners. The consequences of poor learning experiences are too severe to ignore.

The six aforementioned questions touch on the six assumptions of andragogy. Andragogy is a leading adult learning theory that has been evolving and growing for decades. Malcolm Knowles worked extensively with existing theory, along with his own research and ideas to establish how adult learners can best learn. The six assumptions of andragogy are ideas that shape the foundation of how adult learners learn. While many theories regarding educating adults exist, andragogy will be the theory of focus in this text. Without considering these ideas in the design and facilitation of learning for adults, one would be missing opportunities to provide effective and meaningful learning experiences for their respective learners.

Teachers and administrators have a high degree of training and experience around pedagogy, the theory of teaching children. Application of sound pedagogical practices are an expectation in lessons and learning experiences for children. Knowing where children are along a developmental continuum and providing age-appropriate experiences is a responsibility of teachers. This can be successful because a sizable portion of educational experiences that teachers are engaged in during their degree programs focus on pedagogy. Unfortunately, the same cannot be said about andragogy, as it is not a focus of most teacher or administrator preparation programs.

Adult learning theory is not a new concept. German educator Alexander Kapp introduced a term *andragogyk* in his 1833 book.[3] While 1833 may seem like a long time ago, much of Kapp's ideas were based on the teachings of Plato well over 2,000 years earlier. Knowles has worked on andragogy and underlying concepts most of his career and is considered the modern father of andragogy. While the number of assumptions and principles have changed over the years, his structure for and contributions to the science of educating adults has been the standard and should be one of the places someone working with adult learners begins their studies and understanding.

For someone who does not know enough about andragogy and adult learning theory—which appears to be the case with the majority of those in the field of education—the best practices for educating adults begins with the basics. One cannot begin to apply an understanding of andragogy as an adult learning theory without understanding the six assumptions of adult learners. These assumptions have important commonalities and differences when compared with pedagogy. The six assumptions are as follows: the need to know, the learners' self-concept, the role of the learners' experiences, readiness to learn, orientation to learning, and motivation.[4]

The need to know speaks to how adults should understand why something is valuable for them before they start to learn about it. As children in school are taught through the best practices of pedagogy, they often do not have a say in what they are learning about. Children's courses, schedules, and topics are often predetermined. Adults have limited time and more responsibility and, thus, want and need to know why any learning is important before openly engaging in it. Understanding the need as to why they will benefit is a key step in an adult successfully engaging with learning.

The second assumption regarding adults' learning is the self-concept. This assumption is about control. Adults want control over their decisions, their learning, and choices within their learning. As children, these same learners were told what they would be learning and how they would learn about it. Older students in secondary school are often told what courses are mandatory and when to take them. Adults have earned the right in their lives to have choices. Adults not only recognize this but are disappointed when choice is not present. Choice permeates all aspects of an adult's experiences to include what they want to learn about, how, and when.

The third assumption centers around experiences. Adults have a rich set of experiences compared to younger learners. These experiences are built from their family life, the schools they attended, the courses they took, the jobs they have had, and additional choices they made regarding their own personal growth. These experiences can and should be leveraged in their education both by the learner and the facilitator/designer. These experiences have shaped these adult learners, and because of the unique nature of every adult learner, a differentiated and, better yet, individualized learning experience is optimal for meeting adult learner needs.

The fourth assumption focuses on an adult's readiness to learn. With limited time and increased responsibilities as an adult, needs drive their readiness to learn. As adults face needs that meet real-world problems that they have, readiness starts to materialize. Readiness also encompasses all that adults face in their busy lives. An adult may be ready from a knowledge standpoint, but it just may not be the right time in their lives to engage in learning. This assumption has many facets and is personal to the individual adult learner.

This also speaks to the idea of control. If learning is not occurring when someone is ready to meet a need, whether too early or too late, results and outcomes may not reach desired levels. Being ready to learn also implies that the need to know has been met, and if the timing is correct, a self-concept is helped by default. The overlap and connectivity throughout the andragogical assumptions is important to recognize as someone learning about adult learning theory and something to leverage as a designer of adult learning experiences.

The fifth assumption of andragogy is the orientation to learn. This assumption speaks to what type of learning an adult can directly apply to their lives. Adults are motivated to learn what can help them fill a need, solve a problem, or gain a skill to overcome a perceived problem or deficit within their life. This often leads back to a current job and a need that presents itself within that setting. While some learning occurs for periodic growth, most of the learning an adult seeks or is most open to revolves around filling a life-centered need.

The final assumption for adult learners is motivation. There is a shift in the type of motivation that drives a learner as they get older. Young learners are more motivated by external factors. A young child may be motivated by something as simple as a sticker or stamp on their paper. This progresses to the honor roll and similar external kudos that a child might strive for. While adults do respond to external factors such as a promotion or raise in salary, their stronger motivations as they age are internal. Intrinsic motivators such as quality of life and personal satisfaction are proven to be more important to adult learners.

These six assumptions provide a foundation that needs to be understood by anyone who is designing or facilitating learning for adults. Within schools there is a natural deficit of this knowledge by those who are often tasked with professional development. There are commonalities between pedagogy and andragogy, however, as understanding increases it becomes evident that the differences are abundant. So, a principal or teacher leader who has spent their career focused on pedagogy, who is now tasked with providing learning for an adult, will inevitably miss opportunities to intentionally meet adult learners' needs through these assumptions.

Educators are a tough customer when it comes to learning. Yet anyone sitting in a learning environment knows if or when they are having their needs met or not. Regardless of one's knowledge of adult learning theory, they would still know if they were receiving a well-designed learning experience. One must recognize the impact of a poorly designed learning experience on an adult learner and the effect that it can have on future learning events. The outcome of a learning experience can be measured by a change in practice. How does learning designed without attention to adult learning theory leave chances for optimal outcomes?

In the age of social media, most people who are "friends" or "follow" educators will relate to this example. As the school year starts or any time there are in-service days for teachers, posts on social media will rise and contain the following theme. Posts such as "if I was only allowed to just go in my room and teach," "another wasted day of professional learning," or "that was a day I could have better used getting my classroom ready." The words change but the ideas are parallel. Teachers often fail to have their needs met with training or learning experiences that they regularly attend and sadly expect disappointment before the experience starts.

A cynical person could assume that teachers are set in their ways and are not open to change. Yet someone who has been in the system may look at it differently. They might see that learners' needs have not been met. Think back to a high school or college class, a time when learning should begin its shift to a more adult-focused experience. There were classes that clearly met one's needs as a learner and others that did not. The ones that did not were often ones that learners did not want to go to and even dreaded. Has education failed so miserably at providing learning experiences that meet adult learners' needs that teachers have reached this same point?

Culture within a school, district, or state is important. Time is a valued commodity. Preparing for multiple subjects or courses, differentiating instruction, and using research-based strategies are time-consuming strategies. It is a fair assertion that if time is given to teachers for professional learning that the time should offer a positive, impactful learning experience. Whether these experiences occur on a predetermined day without students or require a teacher to write sub plans, time invested deserves a benefit. If time is not valued with positive, well-designed experiences, a culture of not appreciating nor wanting to participate becomes the result.

There is a lot more to adult learning than the six assumptions, however, using them as an early foundation of understanding lets one see what learning should look like at a basic level for adults if they bring the assumptions to the forefront. Designers looking to incorporate the need to know would make sure that objectives are clear and given to participants ahead of any learning events. Explaining the what and the why is always good practice. Providing concrete examples of what the outcomes can and should look like will help the need to know. This could be as simple as showing a video of a practice or strategy in action or sharing samples of student work.

These ideas are not new or revolutionary. However, intentionality in designing learning for adults that differs from learning designed for younger learners should be standard practice. The self-concept is an assumption that if not intentionally incorporated will lead to suboptimal experiences for adult learners. School and district calendars are often made during the second semester for the next school year. Professional learning days are chosen and embedded into these calendars. What this means for adult learners is that a fixed schedule is created for when learning will take place throughout the year and often what that learning will be about.

When the time of learning is fixed and predetermined, self-direction can be challenging. Not all adult learning can easily be categorized. However, for this example, one can create two categories. The first category could be learning an adult chooses. Learning for this category could be but is not limited to an advanced degree, courses chosen to advance a skill, or books and articles that a professional reads. This learning is self-directed and, more importantly, is meaningful for the adult learner. The second category would be learning that is dictated from above. This dictation can be from a supervisor, district, or agency.

Looking closer at this type of forced learning, one must remember that many school and district initiatives are and can be positive. New standards that better address societal needs of students may not be a learning event that a teacher chooses but are important, nonetheless. Similarly, an innovative technology program that is interactive for students, collects student data, or helps manage virtual classrooms may not be a comfortable learning experience for some who do not immediately see a need but can be a positive addition for all stakeholders. Self-concept fits in a gray area because choice is not always possible or easy to incorporate.

How can one incorporate choice and self-direction when not all learners may want to change, see a need for change, or are ready for change? This question again highlights the interconnectedness of adult learning assumptions. While there is no simple solution for helping to address the self-concept in forced learning experiences, there are design aspects to learning experiences that one can incorporate. Choice needs to be the start in any approach to meeting the self-concept. While the goal of learning may be a nonnegotiable, aspects such as where, when, and how learning looks and occurs may be well within the locus of control for a capable designer.

Looking at experiences and how the variety of experiences adults bring to learning necessitates differentiation, the self-concept requires differentiation as well. Tomlinson provides a powerful definition of differentiated instruction, and although it was meant for all learners, it is a natural fit for designing instruction for adult learners. Differentiation should allow for design to meet needs of varied content, process, products, and learning environment.[5] If there is a choice given in any or all of these areas, adults will feel invested in their ownership and self-direction.

Best practices in education highlight the importance of differentiation in content. This should mean the end of one-size-fits-all slide presentations during learning experiences for adults. Those in education know that unfortunately these are still common practices. Adults, like all learners, have different learning style preferences. While there is currently debate in this field as to both the presence and impact of learning styles, if they are perceived by the learner, they cannot be dismissed. How an adult best receives content should be a choice they have so that their needs can be met.

Processes can be linked to the concept of choice and the self-concept by knowing the learning styles of the participants and designing opportunities for learners to engage where and how they are comfortable. Will adults benefit from participating in a hands-on activity? Does the adult need time to process new learning before applying? There are a lot of ways an adult can engage in learning, and the process by which they do should involve some level of choice.

Products can also allow choice. How do learners demonstrate their understanding? It could be through application in a lesson plan or reflection through a journal, the list goes on. Regardless of how an adult does demonstrate their understanding, choice, and the opportunity to have a product related to one's strengths and preferences are both vitally important. Allowing choice increases ownership in the learning process and further engages the adult learner.

If the recent world events of a global pandemic have taught education anything, it is that learning can take place in a variety of settings. While some learners prefer onsite learning experiences where collaboration is at the same table, others may not. Distance learning and self-paced learning will be discussed in great length later in this text. However, knowing that this is a preferred learning method for some adults is important. If using a learning management platform to build learning experiences that can be accessed where and when an adult learner prefers could increase results why would one not want to leverage this type of opportunity?

Allowing choice through a differentiation lens can give power and self-concept to an adult learner when the content is predetermined. Clearly establishing the need to know can mitigate this hurdle while the choices can create ownership. The old excuse of not knowing what one does not know needs to be erased from the mind-set of those working with adult learners. Adult learning theory is not a new area of study. It is simply an area not focused on enough for those entering and in the field of education. Ignorance, budgetary constraints, and missed opportunities in education have left a void and now is the time to fix it.

Adults bring a wide variety of experiences and skills to their positions at a school. These professionals draw from impactful teachers they had in school. The college a teacher attended offered different choices of courses to take compared to another college or university where a colleague may have attended. The person a teacher was paired with as their student teaching supervisor impacted their style and approach. The expectations for lesson planning, the focus of the first school someone works for, and even access to resources shape a professional's experiences and approach to education. The volume of variables that define educators is incalculable.

As previously stated, there are different paths to becoming an educator or an administrator. These differences, as mentioned in more detail in the introduction chapter and briefly summarized here, are a quick yet powerful glance at just how diverse teachers can be. These differences create wonderful opportunities for students to have varying perspectives and skill sets. Yet, one must recognize the creation of broad gaps in knowledge, approaches, and understandings based on this plethora of experiences. With the positive impact a diverse background can bring to a staff, the challenges of gaps from varied experiences cannot be ignored nor underestimated.

A powerful way one can look at this is to study a hypothetical elementary school student. For this, one can identify a fifth-grade student who has attended the same school since kindergarten. For the sake of simplicity, this school contains five teachers at each grade level. This creates five choices for each grade teacher, or 15,625 paths from kindergarten to fifth grade. Those pathways indicate differences in experiences for the student. Imagine the pathways possible from kindergarten through a student's senior year of high school.

This is still just one student in a small school amongst millions of students in thousands of schools. Considering there are almost 24,000 public high schools in the United States alone, one can see just how enormous the number of paths can become. Expand this to include colleges and graduate programs, and the pathways continue to grow exponentially. This further grows as choice in courses, instructors, and programs enter the equation. The elementary example simply calculated different teachers.

While differences are easy to identify and scrutinize, there are notable similarities that our hypothetical student encounters. One knows this student received instruction from the same standards and curricular resources regardless of the teacher they had since schools, districts, and states adopt these. One also hopes grade-level teachers follow best practices regarding collaboration and planning. Depending on the functionality and culture of the grade levels and school, the similarities could outweigh the differences based on their teacher, school, and presence or lack of a collaborative culture.

Adults and their varied experiences look different from a hypothetical fifth-grade student. While having so many differences offer a benefit to learners, these same differences create challenges in adequately addressing the gaps they naturally cause. Educators graduated from different high schools and took varied paths to higher education. These paths may include different colleges and universities, but even if two teachers shared an institution of higher learning, they took different courses, had different professors, and had different student teaching supervisors. All subsequent jobs, supervisors, colleagues, and further education serve to broaden this gap.

With adults having such varied experiences, how can one meet them all to maximize and improve learning outcomes? The honest answer is one cannot meet all the different experiences of adult learners, yet one can meet many. How does that look when designing learning for adults? Knowing one's audience is always the first step. Those fortunate enough to design for groups of learners that they have familiarity with is a beneficial start. This is an advantage that principals and teacher leaders have when working with their own staff. This is a case where relationships and continuity matter.

Forging relationships allows one to know their learners better. Knowing one's learners and leveraging that knowledge to help differentiate is a key advantage that exists in some educational situations with adults and not in others. As mentioned before, principals and teacher leaders with strong relationships have this advantage. Professors can have this advantage, along with an established readiness and need to know from the learner. The key when thinking about differentiation and leveraging experiences is realizing that until those experiences are known and put into context of the learning, one cannot begin to effectively leverage them through design.

Planning for or designing instruction when a relationship exists presents an advantage. On the other side of this, *no* relationship presents a formidable challenge. When an outside professional developer or company representative or even a new principal attempted to engage in learning with a group of adults, assumptions of adult learning can easily go unmet. Jumping blindly into a learning experience under these circumstances is a recipe for missed outcomes. However, well-designed needs assessments can help to mitigate this challenge. A needs assessment could and should be designed to elicit information about the learner's experiences.

The readiness to learn is an assumption that does not fit well with pre-planned or predetermined learning experiences. What are the chances that all faculty members are ready to receive learning on a topic or concept at the same time? Readiness is a challenge in these types of situations. Fortunately, readiness is something that a savvy designer or facilitator can attempt to induce. Often learners are not ready to learn something because they are not fully aware of the benefits or purpose. Demonstrations or videos of the learning in practice, research-based articles, and clear objectives are all ways that readiness can be induced before or during a learning event.

The orientation to learning focuses on life, task, and problem-centered learning. If an adult learner cannot clearly see the purpose of what they are learning and how they can apply it to a problem they face, the learning may not be received nor processed as best as it could be. The approach designers and facilitators should take to meet adults' needs when inducing readiness is to transparently show the benefits and applications of what will be learned, letting participants see early and often why and how learning will benefit them. When the designer clearly focuses on the value of how learning can be applied to the learner's job or life, they are helping create a successful experience.

The orientation to learning seems simple and straightforward. It is, but only if the content is something that can be applied directly to a learner's life. Learning about something important to the employer but not the employee, who is the learner, may not have an opportunity for application and may not be approached in a way that can allow a learner to engage in it fully. This is a content-dependent assumption for the learner. When focusing on school improvement, this can present challenges that a savvy designer will have to try to overcome.

Improvement initiatives are tricky because most if not all of them are chosen to benefit student learning. However, how they are chosen, what strategies accompany them, and how they will be implemented are often not mutually decided with teachers and are often not transparent. This lack of mutual creation and transparency is where teachers can feel like an initiative is done to them as opposed to being something that can benefit them and their practice. If efforts are made to show the value of the application of an improvement effort on student learning so that educators can fully process how it can impact their lives, learning may be more successful.

Motivation is the final assumption one needs to explore to better meet adult learning needs. This is especially critical for learning that was something the learners did not seek. Since andragogy is predicated on adults finding more power in intrinsic motivators, an effective designer of adult learning needs to leverage this. If learning about a new initiative, strategy, or resource can help students be more successful or simply make the learner more effective at their craft, this needs to be clearly and effectively demonstrated and communicated to an adult learner so that they can see this value and use it as an intrinsic motivating factor.

The common thread to all the strategies and approaches to meeting the assumptions of adult learners spans from awareness to an intentional approach. One often gets caught up in what the objective of learning is as the primary driver as opposed to how they should approach their learners, in this case adults, to maximize impact. Thinking about and planning for the adult learner is a necessary practice. However, designing for the assumptions of andragogy into their thinking and approach may be new for many. While only a first step, it is a positive step toward achieving improved gains and outcomes for learning initiatives and experiences.

This is just scratching the surface of adult learning. Other powerful ideas, tools, and models that can and should be explored are the andragogy process model, the practice model, and Kolb's experiential learning cycle. Yet these are only small parts of a big field. Learning more about adult learning best practices and approaches should be the mission of every instructional leader, developer of professional learning, and those who have a role in school improvement. The first step in addressing an issue, in this case, the need for school improvement, is to look at underlying issues. The deficit in adult learning theory understanding and application is a good place to begin.

Progressing further in this text, time will be spent exploring more ways to leverage the basic principles of adult learning theory to help schools. A vast area of focus to think about while working through this problem-solving process is to remember the category of learning. Is the learning mutual and intentionally designed with best adult learning practices in mind or is it a top-down initiative that does not consider adult learning assumptions? If it fits the assumptions of andragogy, then one needs to be intentional in design and apply best adult practices. If it does not, then one needs to find ways for these ineffective learning experiences to improve.

The spirit of this text is to be solution oriented. This chapter speaks to a primary issue, which is a lack of understanding about adult learning theory and basic principles. Hopefully, this chapter gave its readers a brief yet eye-opening look into how adult learners need to be approached differently and intentionally. If it did, then the next question should be, what is one going to do about it? What can an individual, school, district, or agency do to take the next step? The challenge for anyone reading this, regardless of their role, is to be a part of the solution by being proactive in affecting positive change.

Much time was spent focusing on differences that teachers possess. This was to underscore how important design, differentiation, and the assumption that focuses on adult learners' experiences really is. Lack of account for adult learners' needs is only compounded by how different adult learners are. Knowing this information provides both a place to approach improvement as well as an urgency to start that improvement right away.

If the reader is an individual, then the challenge is to learn more about adult learning theory and how one can apply it to their work with educating adult learners. Begin by reading *The Adult Learner, 9th Edition* by Malcolm S. Knowles. If the reader has an influential role within a school, district, or organization, the challenge is to provide opportunities for those who are designing and leading learning for adults to gain a common foundational understanding of best practices in adult learning theory. There is much to be gained from ensuring building and teacher leaders have the necessary tools to be successful.

NOTES

1. Glick, *Instructional Leader and the Brain.*
2. Wolfe, "The Role of Meaning and Emotion in Learning," 35–41.
3. Kapp, *Erziehungslehre, Als Pädagogik Für Die Einzelnen Und Als Staatspädagogik.*
4. Knowles et al., *The Adult Learner*, 43–47.
5. Carol Ann Tomlinson, *Differentiation of Instruction in the Elementary Grades*, 2000.

Chapter 2

Adult Learning Experiences, Not So Fast

Applying knowledge about adult learners, adult learning theory, and best practices in design will help to provide better experiences for learners. Since providing improved learning experiences for adults will help to increase the capacity of any school staff, it is imperative that when given the opportunity to design experiences, one does their best to be intentional regarding best practices in adult learning theory. Nobody sets out to design an inferior experience, but intentionally designing with attention paid to the assumptions of adult learners, using a proven model, and putting pedagogy aside can be the difference between successful learning and falling short.

This chapter will look at why starting with the calendar date and start time of a learning experience is not optimal to affect the desired change. Yes, learning experiences and design need improvements, but before focusing there, an effective designer should begin with a focus on what happens before that experience. When thinking about an adult learner, the assumptions that have been ignored for too long should be at the forefront of planning and designing. This chapter will give the reader a new perspective on how and when in the learning process the assumptions of adult learners should be prioritized.

Good design practices, whether before the learning event or during, begin with the desired outcomes. Regardless of these desired outcomes, a top-down approach to learning for a school staff or individual adult learner will struggle to be effective. One of the most difficult types of learning for a designer to effectively create and execute is one meant for a large group of people (even a whole staff), where the outcomes are predetermined or mandated. District initiatives, school improvement efforts, standards implementations, and new curriculum training, are all examples of times when predetermined goals and outcomes can potentially lead to a poor, one-size-fits-all learning experience.

These large group events, and often top-down experiences, are some of the biggest challenges for most schools and staff. Yet they are also realities for them, and one needs to remain solution oriented. Situations where outcomes are predetermined inherently ignore assumptions of adult learners. Starting with the need to know, one must find ways to be clear and intentional in getting outcomes and benefits for learning to the learners to help them realize their "why." If one is introducing a learning strategy, it is crucial to be proactive in putting information in the learner's hands. This could include providing the learner with videos, samples of student work, or research-based articles.

A mix of clear goals and outcomes, as well as concrete previews in the form of videos and articles, give learners a chance to see the benefits of a new strategy or initiative. Doing this ahead of time also allows for valuable processing time so that learners can think about how this will look in their classrooms, as well as allow time to seek clarification. While it is common practice to have clear goals and outcomes, as well as a snapshot of the strategy at the start of a learning, doing it earlier transforms the timeline of learning experiences. Going from a singular event to a continuous process for improvement is a cultural shift that will benefit learners.

In line with the idea of actions to take ahead of learning, a flexible agenda sent to learners prior to a learning experience can accomplish or strengthen much of what is mentioned in the previous paragraphs. The level of transparency a flexible agenda can provide for learners will help them establish a need to know and can also provide a level of two-way communication that is essential for learners to feel involved in the design process. This concept can get expanded to a flexible and transparent arc of learning for future events that are not discrete and singular in nature. The more access afforded to learners to this information, the more the needs of an adult learners can be adequately met.

The next assumption to make sure that one adequately takes into consideration while planning for learning events is the readiness to learn. Adults are ready to learn when they identify a need for a new skill or knowledge set that will positively affect their ability to do their job or give them a level of improvement. When an outcome or goal is predetermined, let alone the date and time, one is gambling on whether any of the participants have that readiness. It is the designer and/or facilitator's responsibility to better help participants see the value of what will be learned. Similar strategies to how one helps meet the need to know can be employed here.

The idea of inducing readiness to learn is a powerful practice. Inducing readiness is exactly what it sounds like: one intentionally makes efforts for participants to see the value of the learning and how it will be a beneficial and positive experience for them at a given time. This is done through effective communication, transparency, and intentional design. Like the need to know, waiting until the day of the learning experience is, again, not an effective nor proactive approach. With little time to process during learning experiences, even with a strong opening activity, the chance of someone not reaching their readiness is not a good risk to take.

This brings back the idea of shifting the timeline of learning. Learning should be continuous. When learning is simply one event, it is easy for participants to look past what they are doing and not give their full effort. These discrete events are no more impactful than a guest lecturer or a field trip. Shifting both designer and participant mindsets to the idea that learning is continuous is a necessary shift. Starting learning early is an effective way to begin this change. Pre-reads and/or exemplars that contain application of a process or skill are ways to further realize this. A needs assessment that gives participants a preview through questioning is also effective.

One must remember the human aspect of learning. Learners need to be respected and treated as human beings. Tools needed to support learning should be made easily available in order to reduce barriers and show that the learner is respected for his or her time and commitment. Support should similarly be made easily available to learners. Knowing that support will continue beyond a learning event, a series of events or implementation allows a learner to engage with an understanding that their needs will be met. Underestimating the human side of a learner and their needs is a missed opportunity for success.

Adult learners are life, problem, and task oriented around their learning. This is at the heart of the assumption: orientation to learning. This assumption, while tied to the need to know and readiness to learn, speaks more so to a learner seeking engagements that are directly applied to their jobs and lives. In the frame of where learning can be challenging for designers and adults alike, the top-down, directed learning one must lean on the idea of inducing, in this case, the orientation. When the focus of learning is a strategy, initiative, or skill, clearly articulating what it will accomplish and how it will benefit their instructional practice must be accomplished early.

One must recognize, as mentioned before, the overlap in some of the assumptions. Readiness and orientation are strongly connected. While readiness is attributed primarily to a timeframe, there are aspects of the orientation that come into play. Knowing how that application into one's job and life will benefit the learner will allow them to possibly see the need for immediate learning. Planning for intentionality so the learner can see the benefits will open doors for them to become more ready to receive that learning.

When a video is chosen to share with learners prior to the main experience, framing what they will see, why it will be beneficial to their practice, and how it is good for students will help with the orientation to learn. If an article is the method used to help with the need to know and readiness to learn, then providing guiding questions to help frame an orientation to learn will further assist learners in seeing the problem or task it can help them with. Similarly, when student work is provided, a clear background into how the work was produced, how the strategy or initiative was used, and why it helped with the task or problem will help with these assumptions.

Learners can see value in a practice, strategy, or skill by seeing it in action, reading a journal article, or seeing samples of student work. The most effective way to help with the need to know, induce readiness, or orientation will depend on the learners. Differentiating the intentional planning and inductions may be necessary and is a good practice to consider for improving attention to these assumptions prior to learning. Building leaders and local experts need to lean on their relationships with and knowledge of their learners while making sure enough differentiation is occurring to reach all learners.

A crucial benefit of providing information to learners before the learning experience is it creates a discussion point and common foundation with which to follow with a needs assessment. In many cases, the assumption of the role of a learner's experience can be better met after the need to know, readiness to learn, and orientation are established in this proactive manner. Some of the assumptions need to be thought of and approached proactively before the learning event, while others need to still be proactive, yet will occur later in the design phase to be implemented in the main learning event itself.

Regardless of where goals and outcomes are derived from, top-down or jointly, and if that process is in line with best practices, it is essential to intentionally plan for bringing the learners' experiences to the learning activities. How can and will one know what those experiences are? A well-designed needs assessment is the logical place to start. A misstep that is often taken is questions are asked in a self-assessment manner without a common baseline to compare it with. People are asked about their proficiency or comfort with a tool, skill, or strategy, at times using a Likert scale, and the data produced is going to lack validity in measuring proficiency.

If needs assessments are being used to collect data on Likert scales before and after a learning event to show growth, this may fit a need for data but lack a need for adults. Shifting the focus of needs assessments to capture actual participant knowledge and experience is crucial for building appropriate learning experiences. Instead, or in addition to a Likert perception, having participants give examples of their experiences with a tool or process will yield qualitative data that can be leveraged in design. While this benefits the designer, it also frames what is to come for the learner, which is helping to give direction to learning while meeting assumptions.

This is where having a video, article, or student work sample that was used to help with the need to know and readiness to learn can serve as an anchor to bring a common measuring point into a needs assessment. Critical questions can revolve around what was read, watched, or studied. These same questions can tie directly to the objectives and outcomes that are being shared ahead of time so that the language and action words are intentional and clear. Any form of needs assessments can provide data. However, data that will help with prior experience and give an accurate understanding of what the learning is aiming to accomplish is optimal.

Motivation for adult learners favors the intrinsic. It makes sense that if an adult learner sees that a strategy or initiative is good for students and beneficial to their teaching, they will be motivated to learn about it. So how could anyone think that having participants blindly walking into a training room without any prior priming can allow an adult learner to be properly motivated to engage in learning? Sadly, this is common practice and needs to be rethought and adjusted. Thankfully, leveraging the ideas for the need to know, readiness, and orientation mentioned above, along with clear objectives, outcomes, and well-designed needs assessments can help.

Helping an adult with motivation as to why learning will benefit them will change their mindset entering a learning experience. A ready and motivated adult is one who will engage more and will be framing the experiences into how they can apply said learning. Remembering the importance of intrinsic motivation and its role in an adult learner mindset will help the designer be intentional in all pre-learning steps, actions, and decisions. The repeated use of the word *intentional* is included in this text to help those reading understand that the actions and practices chosen by the designer must be done with a purpose and around best practices.

The self-concept is the final assumption that needs discussion at this time. This assumption speaks to adult learners benefiting from choice and self-direction. There are many ways to intentionally plan for choice to better meet adult learners' needs. While this assumption was focused on in the previous chapter, this chapter will frame it a little differently. Choice should be present throughout learning and can look in many different ways. Choice can be as simple as letting participants choose their seats or partners to allowing choice in learning experiences or products to demonstrate understanding. Applying choice in learning experiences allows for self-direction.

Choice is a natural fit when it comes to differentiating learning experiences for diverse adult learners. The intentional and transparent use of choice will help adult learners become ready to accept learning. The idea of transparency is vital. Adults have been conditioned to see a one-size-fits-all agenda as the norm, as if they should feel fortunate enough to receive an agenda at all. Articulating aspects of choice in a flexible agenda that is provided in advance will help and benefit adult learners. Regardless of the where and when learners have opportunities for choice, it is imperative that choice exists, is communicated, and is intentionally designed into experiences.

One easy, early way to involve choice is to bring it into the prelearning. Offer a choice of videos or articles to read. If multiple videos are presented, participants can make an informed decision if the designer includes relevant information, such as the grade level and subject that is featured. Similar approaches can be taken with journal articles and student work. Yet again, the importance of sharing intentionally provided information so that the choice is not blind cannot be understated. Design must be purposeful to help make sure one takes the assumptions of adult learners into account.

Planning and intentionality have been a theme in this chapter that will run throughout this text. Adult learners benefit from the planning and intentionality and from being a part of it. This best practice is often lost due to time constraints or simple ignorance. The more educated those in positions to influence change are regarding best practices of adult learners, the more those best practices can be implemented and realized.

Thus far, this text has spent a lot of time talking not about the learning experiences themselves, but rather what leads up to the actual learning experiences. This time and attention to detail with designing prior to learning is crucial for planning to meet the assumptions of adult learners. The timing and thoughtfulness put into framing the learning experience, whether it is a day or series of events, is important. What precedes learning plays a vital role in the success of an overall learning experience. Taking this time upfront will help ensure that what occurs in the learning experiences themselves has an increased chance of success and meeting desired outcomes.

Chapter 3

Now We Are Ready for Learning Experiences

Now that the learning has been properly framed for participants by giving them foundational information, as well as explaining why it is beneficial and why it fits a need, one can look at designing meaningful learning experiences. At this point goals and outcomes have been introduced and preferably created collaboratively between learner and designer. While it is best practice to have a mechanism to mutually create goals with adult learners, one may be trying to design experiences where outcomes and goals are predetermined. There are still ways to finesse this. Given the goals and outcomes coupled with foundational knowledge, participants can set individual goals.

Knowles' andragogical process model was designed to differ from a typical content model and shift how learning experiences and events are designed for learners. One key difference is that in a content model the outcomes are known in advance and the designer decides in advance what needs to be learned, then designs the order and method of transmission.[1] Content models are centered around a designer and favor pedagogy. The process model centers around a complex topic and adult learners while including design that is collaborative between learner and designer.

Content and process models have a fundamental difference, particularly with the "what" or purpose of the learning experience. This goes beyond the age of the intended audience. A content model is a model designed to disseminate information. This is done through transmission. Transmission can be realized through lectures and PowerPoints. Process models support the design of learning that goes beyond content to actual strategy, skill, or manner of teaching. The appropriate way to help facilitate learning for this would be through modeling and application.

At times there may be a need for some discussion or sharing of information in a more traditional manner, but the primary activities in learning a process do not begin or remain limited to a PowerPoint or lecture. Learning experiences need to keep the focus on the material, the strategy, or the skill that is being taught. This is best achieved through modeling and application. This is especially true for adult learners and how they best interact with and receive new information and processes.

The process model incorporates the following eight steps: (1) preparing the learner, (2) establishing a climate conducive to learning, (3) involving mutual planning, (4) diagnosing needs, (5) formulating program objectives based on identified needs, (6) designing learning experiences, (7) conducting the learning experiences, and (8) evaluating the learning.[2] When thinking about adult learners and their assumptions, it should be reassuring to see that preparing the learner is the first step. If that preparation is done well and intentionally, the data collected when diagnosing needs could double as a mutual planning step.

The previously discussed initial efforts for trying to meet the needs of learners is the ideal way to start work with Knowles' process model. While the model has eight parts, they are not mutually exclusive nor are they meant to be a linear checklist. Some of the prework begins to establish a climate. Climate is a broad concept that goes beyond the temperature of a training room. It speaks to the physical and emotional needs of participants. Climate also speaks to the space, resources, and ability to design with those aspects a positive learning experience for learners. Being mindful of the vastness of climate and designing with intentionality is something within a designer's locus of control.

The climate, which is sometimes referred to as the environment, also speaks to thoughtful planning in order to meet needs. Regardless of the room used, the seating configuration is something that can be controlled so that proximity meets the design to foster collaboration. Environment and climate also speak to resources. This can be as simple as having water and snacks available to meet basic needs of the learners and get more specific to technology access and tools needed for learning. While having the resources available is a first step, having them easily accessible and making participants aware of where and how to access them is equally important.

The climate and environment cannot be fully planned for without considering the human and psychological elements. Learners need to feel safe and respected. For facilitators and designers, intentional effort must be used to make this a reality for participants, and one small misstep can do irreparable damage. Trust is a crucial element of the climate that should not be overlooked. When a large-scale initiative is the setting, fostering trust within the participants is vital. The outcomes, who the facilitator is, and the motives for the learning should be considered during all aspects of the planning and design process to help foster this trust.

Much of the prework attempts to address this trust factor. One's ability and efforts to disseminate information ahead of learning, so that participants know what to expect and therefore become an active part of the planning process through collaboration and/or data-driven decisions, is an important effort. Jumping directly into learning situations without helping create the environment ahead of time is hoping for any level of success instead of planning for a higher level of success. Without knowledge up front and data to drive instructional decisions, one is hoping for readiness. This leads to delivering instruction meant to meet the middle learners while ignoring the rest.

While designers should understand that the primary type of motivation for adult learners is intrinsic by nature, this does not mean that adults do not need an extrinsic reward and motivator at times. Adults positively respond to incentives and rewards when it comes to learning. Rewards and incentives can take many forms. Earning credits toward a degree or pay increases are clearly extrinsic, yet they can be seen as accompanying an internal motivator of self-improvement. Smaller-scale motivators such as verbal affirmations, highlighting of innovative ideas, and tokens ranging from treats to time are all often overlooked, yet effective ways to motivate adults.

An untrained eye when studying Knowles' process model could attempt to fit a group of pedagogy-based learning events and mistakenly think they are correctly utilizing the process model. Trying to employ learning experiences that are not for processes, and yet are specifically designed for adult learners, could erase all the other good elements designed for previously. The learning experiences and design of them should be sequenced by readiness, be focused on problems rather than content, and should be inquiry based. Failing to meet these criteria favors a pedagogy where one needs andragogy as the focus.

Sequencing by readiness shows a commitment to designing around data. It also acknowledges that not all adults can have readiness met before a learning experience starts, yet it is still the responsibility of a designer and facilitator to help have experiences ready to induce readiness at any juncture of the learning process. Educators of children use data regularly to best meet the needs of their learners. They differentiate learning experiences based on data-driven decisions and design experiences to help meet students where they are. This is at the heart of sequencing by readiness. The same best practices in education apply here for all learners.

This also supports the self-concept. If experiences are designed around readiness, then there is a clear dedication to allow choice and attention paid to it during the planning and design phase. This can be articulated to participants throughout the learning so that transparency in design is shared, understood, and appreciated. Showing learners their needs are considered as learning is designed is important. Valuing time spent on a needs assessment and having a level of transparency that speaks to using that or other data in the design process helps connect the learning and design processes.

Learning experiences are still the heart of the process model. How adults are engaged in learning, practice, application, and processing is where one needs to spend considerable time and effort with design. There needs to be engagement, authentic application, and experiences that will meet the varied learners where they are so that everyone can be successful. Participants should leave a learning experience with tangible tools they can take with them. Whether this is a lesson plan, set of organizers, or applicable tools, how can one expect change if learners are not able to take what they learned and apply it quickly and meaningfully?

A critical part of the process model that should not be overlooked is the collaborative nature between the designer and the learners. The process model was intentionally designed to have collaboration between designer and participant throughout. This includes collaboration before, during, and after learning. One way for this to happen, as timing, deadlines, and logistics present challenges, is to maximize the impact of a needs assessment. Designing one that captures how adults prefer acquiring knowledge or skills and how they engage best in activities will help make learning impactful and meaningful to the participants.

Do not let the volume of words from this and the previous chapter given to design aspects of learning experiences be proportional to time spent. Many words dedicated to these chapters focused on prework. This was done to underscore how much prework is typically ignored, yet how much it helps address assumptions of adult learners. Prework is vitally important, yet all the prework in the world will not replace nor make up for pedagogy-based practices where teachers sit and get information. There needs to be considerable time dedicated to planning the learning to include best practices in experiential and applied learning for adult learners.

This type of learning, when designed intentionally, is powerful and effective, but it is also difficult to design and time consuming to differentiate. Hard work and time will yield positive benefits. There is no substitute for the work that is needed in planning successful learning experiences. Educators know this is true with younger students and are not surprised by this for adult learners. Learning about and studying the andragogy process model is a proactive step that those working with adult learners can pair with studying the six assumptions of andragogy.

Keeping with a solution-oriented mindset, how can one provide the best learning experiences for adult learners when they have some control over the design and/or delivery of them? One can give prework the time and attention it deserves. One can keep the six assumptions of adult learners in mind during every step they take while designing learning and learning experiences. One can apply the andragogical process model as a guide to help design experiential learning that will be impactful for every learner. While every designer sets out to do their best to meet adult learners' needs, now they have some tools and models to apply.

The purpose of this text is to focus on improving our schools. This is not an exercise in something that can be easily accomplished through a quick fix. Adult learning theory and its application is a missing but necessary component in many of the nation's schools. The wrong approach to both design and delivery is a hindrance in growth for teachers, which trickles down to students and their ability to grow as learners. When educators without that foundational understanding of best practices in adult learning theory attempt to design and deliver learning experiences for adults, they embark on an uphill battle, destined to fall short of goals.

Hopefully, this chapter provides some insight into how being tasked with providing learning for adults and particularly educators require a major shift in thinking and approach to meet any goals and objectives associated with learning. This chapter and the preceding are far from a complete study of adult learning theory; however, it will hopefully serve as a place to start for those looking to positively impact their colleagues, staff, school, or district. It is never too late nor too frequent to be a reflective practitioner who is solution oriented.

Since so much of the learning that happens at a school is designed and delivered in house, now is the time to start that change. The first step is to identify primary players in designing and facilitating learning experiences meant to benefit teachers and staff. Next, make sure they have a strong and application-based background in adult learning theory, specifically andragogy. However, do not stop there; expand and share that knowledge so all administrators and teacher leaders who may need to apply this knowledge and these processes are a part of a team that can meet adult learner needs.

Most important, anyone involved should continue to build on the knowledge that is shared and gained. Adult learning theory is a vast and complex area of study. Committing to a continuous learning process is a step forward. Educators have dedicated a long time in their careers focusing on pedagogy and young children. This is a difficult mind shift and one that will come with growing pains and require support. What cannot get lost is this shift is focusing on adult learning theory to help support learning experiences, which will help schools improve and most importantly benefit children.

NOTES

1. Malcolm S. Knowles et al., *The Adult Learner*, 51–71.
2. Knowles et al., *The Adult Learner*, 51–71.

Chapter 4

Human Resource Development

This chapter will focus on exploring education and improvement from a different lens. This text would be missing a valuable opportunity if it did not look at some roles and structures within schools from a business perspective. This will not be a talk about budgets. However it will explore roles and responsibilities of leadership, where they tend to be, and where one should want them to be. This will also include an exploration of the concept of human resource development (HRD). This broad topic speaks about maximizing one's human assets. One may see dissonance between these ideas and some of the best practices in adult learning theory. Keep an open mind while looking for solutions from multiple perspectives.

Education is often a field where jargon changes, yet ideas tend to be a little more stagnant. If one has been in education long enough, they have witnessed the endless repackaging of ideas, initiatives, and strategies. The content is virtually identical, but the buzz word, or acronym, is new. A renewed push to adopt or utilize something is made with fanfare as if the "new" thing is the answer to all of one's problems. One idea that rings true to this observation is the title used for a building leader, a principal, an instructional leader, an administrator, and so forth. The list goes on. One such current flavor of the week is to call principals "instructional leaders."

Principals wear many hats. They are administrators in every sense of the word. Administrative duties and functions take up a sizable portion of a principal's time, effort, and attention. While administrator is not a sexy name for the job done by a principal, it is an accurate one. Schedules, budgets, discipline, supervision of students and adults, safety, and so much more are primary duties. As more initiatives are pushed down from above, the less time an administrator has to be an instructional leader. Yet, this is a term that is chosen to signify a commitment to better instruction, leading by example, and providing support needed to teachers and staff.

In a perfect world the position of principal would embody what it means to be an instructional leader. The principal would spend their days in classrooms.

They would be helping with lessons, co-teaching, and working directly with students and teachers. They would have opportunities to provide actionable feedback to teachers and staff and regularly follow up with them. Principals would be directly involved with coaching cycles, instructional rounds, lesson planning, feedback protocols and data sessions to help drive instruction. Yes, principals are involved in these activities, but are they involved enough to dynamically impact positive change?

This example of both the terminology and the best intention attempt where one knows what someone could or should do in an ideal situation but is limited due to restrictions and other factors, is a microcosm of other similar realities in education. The primary purpose of this text is to look at ways to alter approaches to improving education. Sometimes simply looking and reflecting is overlooked yet needed. Would a true instructional leader make a school perform better if given the opportunity to do all the aforementioned activities as often as needed? Most would resoundingly say yes.

The introduction highlighted the impact an above-average principal can have on student learning compared to a below-average principal. The gain in student learning a highly functioning principal can yield is too important to ignore. Effective principals are actively involved in more than just the administrative side of the job and are given the opportunity to enact change where it is required given their unique situation and school needs.

Earlier this text focused on andragogy, what it looks like, how it can improve learning for adults, and how there is a deficit of knowledge around andragogy in people who could benefit from knowing more. What if andragogy was not always the best choice regarding all learning that adults engage in within a school setting? Just as the term "instructional leader" may not be the most accurate or honest term for a principal, maybe andragogy is not the most appropriate approach in all done to educate adult learners. This may sound like a contradiction, but if one has learned anything in education it is that they know that differentiation is a best practice.

The focus of HRD is the improvement toward goals within an organization. While definitions vary, the common theme around HRD is increasing or improving skills, knowledge, and/or capacity. This usually takes place within an organization or population. One can even look at the process of education as a whole as a function of HRD. Sending children to school is a way for society to improve skills, knowledge, and capacity. While this is important to recognize, this text will focus on the adult side of HRD.

To get more specific, HRD can be seen as a subset of both human resource management (HRM) and human development. Human resource management is a larger umbrella that goes beyond improving and includes hiring, recruiting, and retaining talent. Human development focuses on improving the quality of life. When putting these two more broad fields on the table, one can see how HRD easily and naturally is a subfield or subset of both. Improvement is central to the aspects of both human development and human resource domains.

Human resource management and development are fields schools utilize, albeit in different ways. Schools and districts have a mission and vision. Schools and districts set goals, and both use data to determine goals and measure their progress. This process can happen at small levels such as for individual students or classrooms and grows in scope to occur at departments, grade levels, schools, and organizations. Yet when one looks at the idea of improvement, what does that really look like in the context of the adults who are the direct conduit to students and their growth?

Before moving forward, it would be prudent to take a step back. While all six assumptions of andragogy are important, one should take a minute to refocus one's thinking around the idea of the self-concept. The self-concept focuses on the idea of choice and self-direction within an adult's learning. The need for self-direction is important for adults, and having the opportunity for self-direction and choice in their learning is the key to the proper mindset and openness to learn. Adults having the opportunity to choose their learning path, how and when they learn or what they deem as important to learn, is a recipe for them maximizing their learning outcomes.

Are there any potential problems with this? People choose learning that speaks to them, fills an internal need, helps reach a goal, or is a part of a large sense of self-fulfillment. Will this learning that is self-directed by an adult in the education field necessarily be in line with a larger organizational (school, district, or system) initiative or need? Education institutions usually require a certain amount of professional learning to occur during a licensure renewal cycle, however the requirements for what is accepted vary widely and rarely connect cohesively to specific organizational initiatives.

Choice and self-direction, which are important to the adult learner, both for starting learning and successful outcomes, can often move a learner away from an organizational need and toward their own goals and needs. While on a personal level this sounds positive for the adult, it can widen gaps in knowledge systemically. If all teachers simply build their own capacity in areas they want, how can a system or organization cohesively improve? Obviously, there will be some opportunity for common learning experiences at a school level, but if those do not represent a sizable portion of one's learning and fail to represent the assumptions of andragogy or are not chosen by the learner how effective can they be?

Now reflect on the need to know and readiness to learn. The need to know is an understanding of why and how learning will have a positive impact on someone, and readiness is a personal state of acceptance of new learning. While choice, understanding, and readiness only represent half of the assumptions of adult learners, they represent a big part of what is often missing when adults are presented with learning they did not choose. How can one expect learning to be effective if it fails to meet assumptions of andragogy? Why would one invest time and effort in what is seemingly a losing battle?

Trying to approach this issue from a lens of best intentions, one can see where things went wrong. Having schools that simply allow teachers and staff to determine their own learning paths and hoping this can positively impact the school seems unrealistic. While this may result in learning that has met more assumptions of adult learners, it also could lead to learning occurring that does nothing to address underlying deficits within the school or gaps in knowledge of skills possessed by the staff. What if students are specifically struggling with writing or with modeling in mathematics? Can or will fully self-directed learning effectively and systematically address this in the scope of a school, district, or organization?

This is where one needs to step away from andragogy for a minute to look at what one is really trying to accomplish. Just as any organization, education, or business, one wants to maximize the instructional impact, or in a business sense, the return on investment. In an educational context that would have someone hiring and retaining the best talent, human resource management, while helping to build their skills and capacity to best meet the unique needs of the student they work with, human resource development. Can one see the dissonance that exists between how adults best learn and what would be best for schools and students?

Building skills, knowledge and capacity of children is a basic function of HRD. Building skills, knowledge, and capacity of adults to provide the best education for children is a basic function of HRD in an educational context. This will inevitably involve adults engaging in learning that they may not choose. The same holds for learning that is not something that they fully understand the need for nor are ready for at the time of a learning event. While readiness is something a savvy designer can help induce for adult learners, one must shift their thinking to a systems approach matching an organization or business model.

This text is not meant to point fingers at anyone. There are no singular reasons or people to blame for the need to improve our schools. However, in the same effort of being solution oriented, everyone can be leveraged to help reach the goal. This begs a simple question, do all adults in education realize their role within the big picture, and do all adults in education fully remember why they do what they do? For many or most this question will get a resounding yes. However, for some, this creates an opportunity. Being reminded of one's purpose and how it aligns or fits with a system's mission and vision should never be taken for granted.

In a business approach, everyone and everything would be considered assets. They would be looking to maximize capacity, maximize productivity, and maximize the outcomes. In a business the company would still establish a mission and vision. They would set goals and targets, and provide employees with learning, resources and support needed to achieve the goals and targets. Achievement would be celebrated and failure to achieve would be met with change. This sounds cold or sterile, but it is a system of expectations, approaches, and accountability. Does one hear more about successful, well-run companies or about successful, well-run schools?

While many differences exist, there is one substantial difference between the business world and education that requires extensive discussion. A business has the freedom and ability to hire who they want; restructure as needed and change their focus as appropriate. The education world, especially the public sector, does not have this level of control. If one were to start a business, they would hire specific people for specific functions. They could determine salaries based on needs, skills, and performance. They could adjust the size and scale of departments based on dynamic factors. This ability to design is powerful.

These advantages that businesses enjoy go beyond the human workforce. Companies can choose the best resources and technologies that fit their needs and vision. Technologies, platforms, and systems can be custom made to fit these unique needs and can be adjusted or changed when there is a need to do so. One can find the best space, office configuration, and make changes as needed. Businesses are rarely limited or tied to a specific geographic area and when it is time to move locations to fit needs, it is as simple as finding a better location and space.

Look at a similar yet different scenario. Someone is hired as the principal of a large public school. While theoretically they are the building supervisor, the instructional leader, the agent of innovation and change, how much of an impact can they have compared to that of a leader of a company? Their workforce is predetermined by a staffing formula that will allow so many positions based on the student population and funding considerations. They are further bound by a staff that has been chosen by someone else before they arrive. They will have younger and older staff members with a varied skill set and various commitments to the school.

The physical school they have inherited will inevitably have improvement projects already in place. There will be needs that will not be able to be addressed during the current budget cycle. This new administrator will be learning about the physical needs, what will be possible to fix, and what needs attention as time in the building increases. They will have to prioritize projects and initiatives based on funding and immediate needs. The student population can change at any moment. There will be impacts on needs and the physical space based on these fluctuations. So much of what principals face is out of their control, as opposed to those who lead a business.

Everyone has a picture of an ideal teacher in their mind. While each might have a slightly different wish list for their traits and abilities, there are some commonalities. Common threads are someone with experience, a strong background in their content area, a desire to continually improve their craft, and most importantly, cares about students. One hopes, and at times assumes, that every school in America is full of these dynamos, yet that is not necessarily the case. When given the opportunity, teachers often choose where they can make more money, teach the types of courses and classes they want to teach, and do so in a location that fits their life needs.

So, for this theoretical building leader, here is a summary of some of the challenges that they face. They enter their new job with a staff that has been chosen without their input. This staff could be amazing or could be less than stellar. It will take time to figure out the staff's strengths and weaknesses and how to best utilize their workforce to meet student needs. They will have to learn the best practices that are common for the staff, as well as what initiatives they follow with fidelity. They will have to learn the intricacies of the building, grounds, and how the space fits the needs of the school's programs and students.

Most importantly, they will have to learn about the students. No two schools in America have identical student populations and the underlying school culture further changes with their unique attributes and needs. So, as a school leader, one has a lot to navigate about how they can best meet the abundance of needs that exist and are able to identify. The owner of a business can target populations for their product or service, but a school leader cannot do that. The students in their population are not people one can nor should want to pick and choose to serve.

It seems the more one compares a business and a school, the more one sees their differences as opposed to their commonalities. However, someone needs to look no further than the fact that both have the purpose of maximizing their ability to affect change and meet goals. Putting differences aside, they are systems that function with a purpose. That purpose is primarily people-centered with a desired outcome of continually improving. Resources are allotted to help make necessary changes and improvements to better accomplish goals. Human resources are some of the greatest resources that are in the locus of control of improvement.

This again brings one back to the idea of human resource development and how it fits into the big puzzle that is improving schools. Regardless of the litany of budgetary barriers that schools face, existing staff members, diverse abilities of staff members, and the student population, one needs to be solution oriented. In the business world, if learning needs to occur, workers learn and improve or face the real possibility of consequences that could include not having a job. This is an oversimplified and punitive view of HRD in business, but the world of business is competitive and often that competition creates a hunger to both improve and please.

Why is it then that education functions so differently? School improvement is often met with resistance and skepticism. Personal improvement is often more important to people in the education field than systemic improvement. Tenure, which serves as a great incentive for people to join the education profession and serves to help keep control over who can be dismissed from their job, also has a negative effect of protecting some teachers who maybe have not given their all to systemic improvement efforts. The differences between business and education again seem more abundant than similarities.

How can a building leader effectively leverage human resource development for the betterment of all stakeholders in a school community? Furthermore, what can a school look like that does this effectively? To answer these questions, one needs to dig deeper into what steps they would need to take to effectively change and improve a school. One would need to know the skills and deficits of all employees. They would have to know the needs of the current student body. They would need to know the available resources to affect change. Finally, they must know how to best put this together into a flexible and achievable plan.

Knowing the skills and deficits of all employees in a school is something that will take time and intentional effort to uncover. An instructional leader who only visits classrooms once or twice a year could never fully know the strengths and weaknesses of their staff. This would take frequent and regular visits to see teachers and staff working in different capacities, with different groups of students, and do this often enough to discern patterns. Most teachers can put on a dog and pony show when they know a formal observation is scheduled. This helps nobody. An instructional leader needs to be present often enough to see the full reality.

This goes back to what was discussed earlier. The instructional leader needs the uninterrupted time and opportunity to effectively lead instruction. If this is not possible, one cannot expect to affect change or improve schools. There also needs to be an open-door culture at a school and one where there is a safe, trusting, and respectful climate between leadership and staff. Until that is established, little to no impact will occur. In the spirit of being solution oriented, the instructional leader should possess the people skills to build trust and earn respect with their staff in order to create a culture of open doors and transparency.

Now that the strengths and weaknesses of the staff are known, one can identify common practices, common needs, and some next steps for systematic improvement. This must be paired with the unique student needs of that school. Complete and continuous data analysis will need to occur. This process must be continuous because needs will evolve as new data points are studied and chosen strategies are measured for their effectiveness. Students should be the center of all efforts. The purpose of human resource development is not to change the clients—in this case the students—but to provide support and help the staff to meet goals and objectives.

Having and analyzing data to help effectively improve and grow as a system is vital. That data includes where teachers and staff are, as well as where students are. This will lead to what strategies and actions one needs to impact the learning that occurs. Keep in mind, this is not work for the sake of accreditation. This is a continual process led by the building's instructional leader. Of course, they will leverage expertise wherever they can to effectively carry out this work, but the lead needs to come from the head of the school, district, or organization and then be collaboratively shared with all stakeholders.

If this process is done well, through an intentional and transparent effort, all stakeholders, especially the teachers and staff, will be ready to learn whatever is needed to affect this change to benefit students. Remember the importance of teachers embracing their role in the school, district, and/or organization. This learning may be centered around instructional models, best practices, strategies, or a combination of all three. However, it is important to focus on the intentionality of the process. Some will say that all schools do this. One needs to recognize that all schools do some version of this but get misguided along the way. Results speak for themselves.

If leadership does not have a complete and accurate picture of the skills and deficits of each staff member, and if they do not have an accurate picture of student needs, improvement is not going to occur at an optimal level. Furthermore, if teachers and staff are only learning about what they want to learn about and not what the organization focuses on systematically, then the school cannot move forward in an intentional manner. In the spirit of adult learning, if the need to know and readiness are not fostered intentionally, the adult learners may not be invested. Finally, if the expectation to move forward as a unit is not clear, change will not happen.

So yes, every learning institution uses elements of good practice for improvement. However, it is the combination of giving leadership the fair opportunity to lead the effort without being weighed down by minutia, employing some best practices of adult learning theory and marrying that with a human resource development approach that can transform how schools operate. When a school gets to the place where shared learning is both the expectation and culture, then real change can concur. It should be the underlying goal to get teachers to think like the people in business who want to learn what is deemed as best for the organization.

This type of shared learning and ownership of students as a system is the way forward for schools to improve. But again, this is where one must shift their thinking to human resource development. What is most important in a school? The students are and therefore should be the focus of all that is done. If students are the focus, then meeting their needs systemically is the path forward for teachers and administrators alike. This should and could change how evaluation occurs both among teachers and administrators. While the word "evaluation" makes some nervous, how else can one effectively measure what is being done?

Teachers should be evaluated not solely on test scores or how nice a single lesson looked during a scheduled observation. Teachers should be evaluated on their ability to systemically fit into the school's direction. If the right data is used and the necessary resources are provided, then one has a recipe for school or organizational improvement that should be followed in order to do what is best for the particular student population that is served by a school. This would create a unique manner in how they are developing the human resources, the teachers, and staff, for each school. Unique development would require specialized evaluation.

Imagine trying to measure the effectiveness of a process that may or may not be fully implemented. If a company were to adopt an efficiency plan, they would only measure the impact of that plan or resource once they knew that employees were using it. Imagine a similar scenario in a school. If a deficiency were noticed in data points and a specific strategy or tool could address it to help students, one would not start to measure student growth until the teachers had the training, resources, and then implemented the strategy or tool. Yet there are gaps in this type of process in schools that exist more than one would want to admit.

Developing human resources, especially the ones that were not necessarily chosen nor hired by the current leader, should be a top priority of any school or organization. Developing them in a meaningful and continuous manner is the way forward to helping realize actual change and improvement in schools. The processes and ideas mentioned in this chapter are not new. However, viewing it through the lenses presented may be a different approach than some are used to. Keeping priorities student centered and organizationally focused is imperative. However, change is not easy and takes time, consistency, and commitment.

Teachers can still grow personally and professionally in areas that they identify. Systemic learning should not be the only learning that teachers engage in. However, being a part of a bigger purpose and system is something teachers should embrace and not push back against. Teachers have a commitment to serving students and the stakeholder community for whom they work. That commitment includes systemic growth to achieve school and system goals. This commitment also includes personal growth to improve one's craft. Everyone who chooses education should understand this as a part of the obligation.

Schools should be transparent with their processes and direction for human resource development. This information should be made easily available to all stakeholders and prospective hires. When leadership employs a transparent approach with all intentional efforts, everyone benefits. This transparency will help potential staff and the ones doing the hiring to find the best fits in an effort for the most successful partnerships possible. This is a missing component regarding regular hiring practices in education.

Human resource development should also be a priority for principals and those above them. Principals should be given the resources and tools to analyze data, be present in the building and classrooms, and lead a collaborative effort for building improvement. Principals should not just be evaluated by test scores or discipline statistics. They should be evaluated on how well they create the systemic plan for their school and how well they provide their teachers and staff the resources and tools necessary to be successful with this implementation. Principals should have high-level knowledge of adult learning theory.

Principals should also be evaluated on their ability to attract, hire, and retain talent within their school. They may have limited ability to change an existing staff, however, their ability to make the working climate a place of trust and respect will help to both attract and retain the teachers and staff that can have the biggest positive impact on the school. This human resource development and management approach to leading a building is the direction that can lead to impactful change in schools. Again, this hinges on allocating the time and resources needed for all to properly do their job and do it the way it needs to be done.

While building leaders are often evaluated by test scores of students, why not also include the growth of their teachers? If the building leader is the instructional leader and is the one who helps with systemic learning, they should own their staff's growth. If they are collaborative in improvement efforts, transparent in direction, and have a staff that employs systemic thinking, that growth will be realized. This growth will lead to student success. Is this not the work that should be the basis for measuring how dynamic an instructional leader is?

As stated before, the purpose of this text is not to rebuild schools from the ground up. This is both unrealistic and unnecessary. The purpose is for learners to look for ways to maximize what one can do with what they have. Furthermore, it is to reexamine what they are doing and why it is not working more efficiently. It is a time to look in the mirror and ask how to impact change. The ideas in this chapter are not a major shift from current ideal practices yet could be closer or farther from the realities of any given school or institution.

All schools can benefit from a renewed approach to continuous improvement. One can label a public high school as being successful if it has high attendance rates, strong standardized test scores, and high graduation rates. However, how much and how far can someone track the ultimate success of those students? How successful are those same students in higher education, in the workforce or as citizens in their communities? This speaks to the secondary level of human resource development that is a product of the HRD within a staff and system.

While many of the changes in a school through a human resource development approach are in practices and strategies, there are always dominoes that fall. For instance, if a principal is going to serve as an actual instructional leader and evaluator of human resource development, then someone else may have to help carry out the other lengthy list of duties that most principals are charged with. This will result in some reassignment of duties and reclassification of responsibilities within schools. Assistant principals may become the budget and discipline lead. Some schools have solutions for this already, and others may need to examine and implement something new.

Regardless of the place that each school is in, it is time to look at making sure that one is doing what they say they are doing. If a principal is to be an instructional leader, then someone needs to provide them with the tools and resources to be just that. If one is going to effectively use data to drive decisions and support learning initiatives, then one needs to both do that and provide the support to all staff to realize any changes that need to occur. If one needs support with data analysis, then they may need to leverage local resources. If one is going to change how they evaluate professionals in a systematic manner, then one needs to do it for the whole system.

Change takes time, but it starts with a clear vision of where one wants to go. It also starts with honest evaluation and recognizing the problems that exist while taking a solutions-oriented approach to improvement. Using a human resource development mindset in education is a small step that can yield big results. While there is some dissonance between the assumptions of andragogy and systemic learning, some middle ground can be found with transparency, the right climate for learning, and strong leadership. This is but one step of many in improving education, but if done well, the students will be the ultimate beneficiaries.

Chapter 5

Local Resources

While teachers and administrators may not all currently be experts in adult learning theory and how to best meet the educational needs of teachers and staff, there are experts within the community that are often not fully leveraged. Colleges, community colleges, and universities house education departments. These education departments are comprised of professionals that spend their time working with adult learners, have a background in the best pedagogical and andragogical practices, and have access to the latest research about education. These institutions also have undergraduate and graduate level students that can offer valuable support to local schools.

Partnerships already exist between higher education institutions and some local school systems. There are established programs for college interns to complete their student teaching experiences at local schools. The program's main purpose is to allow college students to gain experience in a school and classroom. This experience is vital for aspiring teachers to learn the necessary balances between planning, classroom management, and best practices of pedagogy. However, as student teachers come and go in and out of local schools, the lasting impact they have on the schools they visit is minimal.

Higher education also contributes to local schools, teachers, and the local education community in other ways. This can include workshops, symposiums, grants, and other financial and educational support. Workshops can provide timely learning opportunities for local educators to attend. These workshops allow experts within higher education to share new advances, technologies, or techniques. They also allow partnerships to form with local teachers connecting with each other and also connecting to those organizing and leading the workshops. Symposiums offer similar opportunities for the sharing of learning and connections.

Grants, technology sharing, and other financial support allow higher education to give to and partner with local schools. Grant programs allow local schools and their workers to find an opportunity to get financial support that is not available within their normal budget. Technology sharing allows another chance for resources to be utilized by local schools. Many higher education institutions also allow training to accompany this technology. The point of bringing up student teachers, workshops, and financial support is to highlight that strong partnerships exist. However, regarding improvement, more can be done.

How can one leverage college and university departments to help schools be more successful? What if one started by leveraging a two-way relationship between higher education and local schools and systems. While partnerships exist, many can be one-directional. What if schools could utilize the abundance of resources available at a higher education institution? These resources span from statistical analysis, rethinking focused school-improvement initiatives, as well as research support. These partnerships can happen with any higher learning institution.

What if data analysis at a school level was given support from a statistics department? Yes, those in education analyze data on a regular basis, however, are they as skilled at analyzing data and drawing conclusions as someone with a background in statistics? The phrase "data rich, information poor," or sometimes "data rich, analysis poor" is a cliché in education. This speaks to the abundance of data points that teachers and schools have access to yet fail to fully analyze and leverage. Yet, if data analysis happened in an efficient manner, more students would have their needs met. Imagine the impact that better and more frequent analysis could have.

If there were true statisticians supporting school data analysis, this could make revolutionary changes to how schools operate. Allocation of resources could change based on data. School goals and areas of focus could be based on higher-level data analysis and more focused support could be put in place. School action plans are and have historically been the result of data analysis. But has anyone looked at how accurate that data analysis was? Is anyone scrutinizing not just the process that is school improvement but more importantly, the execution? Everyone has room to grow, and a statistics-based partnership is a small step.

This does not have to be placing the burden of analyzing statistics on the few statistics professors at a college or university. Why could students studying statistics not be leveraged for this partnership? A systemic process could be employed where the information needed to analyze a data set could be submitted to a local college and university. This data set is then passed along to the capable student or professor to perform a valid statistical analysis and create a report for the school. This fits two needs: a better analysis of statistical data for schools and applied analysis opportunities for university and college students.

If a university is large enough to house a full statistics department, there could be more opportunities to leverage. For public universities and colleges, why could one not create additional positions to help with this purpose? The benefit of improved teaching and learning at local communities should be enough to justify a few positions that could benefit multiple schools, which would equate to impacting thousands of students. The alternative to having the most knowledgeable people doing the analysis is the potential for wrong or incomplete analysis and interpretation and basing resources and time toward those potentially flawed findings.

Some districts in the country have a statistical expert or educational researcher with the sole responsibility of data analysis. Yet many schools do not. Does having a degree in statistics necessarily make for a smooth transition dealing with available data points within a school? Could practical, applied opportunities help learning in college? Bridging this gap to help create equity and access to improve analysis practices would benefit all parties involved. Misinterpretation of data and a lack of ability to interpret data are real problems in schools, yet solutions can be easier to find when looking in the right place. Why limit college and university support of schools to the education department when natural fits of mutual benefit can be fostered elsewhere? This could finally put an end to the idea of schools being data rich and analysis poor.

Student teaching is a program built into education majors to get teaching candidates authentic and applied experience with students in a classroom. Students take a practicum course where they are paired with a local school and teacher to work side by side for a semester honing their skills as they work toward their degree. Some programs will have students doing a form of a practicum during their sophomore, junior, and senior years. Other colleges and universities limit this to one or two opportunities. Regardless, this experience is varied and could be leveraged more effectively to benefit all parties.

Schools and districts along with their partner colleges and universities can take additional steps to make these practicum experiences more beneficial for all parties. Schools have initiatives and strategies integral to school improvement and district priorities. The teachers in those schools have attended training and professional learning in attempts to help embed understanding and practice in classrooms. However, these strategies and initiatives are nowhere to be found for college students who enter these buildings to do their student teaching. Why is the partnership not a two-way endeavor?

Best practices and strategies employed by local schools near colleges and universities could produce much more classroom-ready teachers if they exposed their students to specific strategies and initiatives that are used in local schools. This benefits everyone. Local institutions of higher learning would be turning out young professionals who bring a ready skill set to local schools and districts that match specific areas of focus. Young professionals can market themselves as knowing and being able to apply skills that are best practices and research based beyond content specific and general pedagogy practices.

One of the greatest benefits of this type of practice is instructing an adult when they are ready to be taught. Students in college have a need to know and a readiness in line with assumptions of adult learners. They are taking these courses mostly by choice and want to be successful so that they can find jobs. It could be easily argued that any learning done in a college or university setting would be more effective compared to learning done on professional-development days in a school or district setting because the assumptions of andragogy are better met and those delivering and designing the instruction have more practice with adult learners.

Imagine new teachers walking into a school on the first day, ready to contribute to a set school culture where they can and will apply a common writing strategy, being versed in a specific data analysis protocol, or simply have the tools to do more than be a new teacher trying to establish themselves. Much of the focus of any education program in a college is a mix of broad content. This looks different for perspective elementary and secondary teachers.

Elementary teachers take courses in all areas of content to get ready for teaching all core subjects. Secondary teachers have what can amount to a double major in a content area and in education. If the program does not offer a double major, it is still close to one. However, some of the practical strategies, protocols, and areas of focus used in actual schools are often ignored in traditional coursework.

Education majors get a lot of information in their programs but unfortunately, it is a small amount of information on a lot of topics and ideas. A secondary math teacher will get a robust mathematics background far beyond what they will teach. Yet, they will take teaching methods courses, pedagogy courses, courses on special education, reading, and depending on the institution, a few other education courses of varying topics. Prospective teachers are given some tools through regular coursework to be successful but anyone who has been through this knows that the student teaching experience is really what puts it all together.

Here is the opportunity. Having parts of that student teaching experience include learning about specific methods, strategies, and initiatives that mirror the school's. This is a best practice of differentiation. Could all elementary teacher candidates who are participating in student teaching not benefit from both learning about specific initiatives of the schools they are working at as well as learning about specific initiatives of other schools that their classmates are working at? This gives them tools to take forward into their future jobs and gives them a realistic and a strong glimpse of what directions schools and districts are taking to inform job decisions.

These types of two-way partnerships are mutually beneficial. If teaching strategies and initiatives are being taught in the local institutions of higher education, could this not be further leveraged into that institution giving back to their communities by offering continuing education courses on those same initiatives? Could they not offer both online and face-to-face instruction and workshops to the community to help build more capacity and do so with instructors who have backgrounds in adult education and adult learners? Might these offerings appear more valuable to teachers who want a positive learning experience?

Building on the idea of bringing support from colleges and universities to statistical analysis of school data to drive school improvement is a next step. Teachers and administrators have a limited knowledge of what is new and current based on their time and access to research. Higher education is already conducting much of this research and has a pulse on what is current and effective. What if education departments and graduate students—who have more time than one's average teacher or building leader to conduct research—could make applied projects out of matching current-research-based best practices and strategies with the needs that data identify?

This further leveraging of local resources and partnerships is an exciting way to pair researchers and practitioners in education. What if new tenure-track requirements for college professors in statistics and education fields made partnerships a part of their requirement for getting and retaining tenure? While in a perfect world one would want this to be a voluntary partnership, sometimes requirements help get more people involved and build systemic practice. Regardless of how this starts, the power of involving colleges and universities in the local school processes of school improvement cannot continue to be overlooked.

The details behind how this begins, sustains, and grows are not what is important at this stage. What is important is identifying potential resources that could and quite frankly should be leveraged to help improve schools. There are experts and leaders in education well versed in budding research and innovation. While there are passionate teacher leaders and educational leaders in schools, their access to what is current is limited to what professional journals they subscribe to and who they follow on social media. Those in higher education simply have more access and, thus, a better chance for meaningful impact.

Leveraging this access and expertise is not a failure on the part of principals or teachers. There should be a "work smarter, not harder" mindset, and knowing where to find help and support is not a straightforward process in education. Those in education are tasked with many things and are asked to do a lot. Knowing where and how to outsource some of the work is not something that comes naturally to everyone. With time being the most valuable commodity, and with a focus on being solution oriented, it is time to start looking for better ways of doing things.

Students in all grades, from elementary to middle to high school, engage in research. Research is an important part of ELA standards, and using evidence from text is seen throughout those standards. Again, looking at undergraduate and graduate programs, students, professors, as well as librarians, one has many local opportunities for new partnerships. Public libraries and college and university libraries can offer access to databases, professional journals, and valuable knowledge on how to search, access and cite evidence from text. The power of technology can bring these resources as close as they need to be to help access, expand, and normalize.

School libraries should expand partnerships with public libraries and public college and university libraries. Finding ways to bring more books, eBooks, research journals, and periodicals to the hands of administrators, teachers, and students in all grade levels is only going to further benefit teaching and learning. This does not need to be a physical partnership. Finding ways to access online resources is not only possible but should be a priority. In an age of information, why should anyone limit the information that people, especially those in education, have access to? If local libraries are for the same public that schools service and higher learning institutions are public, why not expand access?

This access should not be limited to informational resources. Everyone should be looking at using technology to bring human resources to students. Public librarians could be partners with schools and have access to what is being studied and researched in local schools. School library hours are limited much more so than public libraries. Why are people not working together better so that public libraries are reinvigorated as places where learning continues? Could book, periodical, and technology resources be organized to better support what schools are working on? Why would anyone not want to strengthen partnerships to better benefit the larger community?

Do not lose sight of the reciprocal benefits of stronger partnerships between academia and the field. One of the weaknesses of academia and being at a university or college is that while research is a part of the job, the practical application and work in the field is lacking. While research has incredible value in any area of study, being too far removed from any real setting broadens the gap between theory and application. This creates a separation between those in the field and those doing research about the field. It also brings a level of mistrust where people in the field do not think someone that is far removed from practice can help them.

The converse proves true for those doing the work, the teachers, and the administrators. Often many in education, once they have earned the degrees they want or are motivated to earn, spend less time doing research, learning innovative ideas, and staying on the forefront of educational innovation and best practice. Since much of the new or current ideas live in academia and research journals. Access to them, while not limited, is limited to those with the need to know or who are ready to learn. Those without the motivation, need, or readiness are away from that access and miss opportunities to learn from them.

The mutual benefit of more partnerships is that access comes back to those in the field, and those in academia are given access to what is happening in the field. A professor who focuses on pedagogical best practices in their courses needs to know and be current with the types of tools and resources being used in classrooms. They also need to know current realities in today's students. Having this knowledge and being able to teach about it not only benefits all parties involved, but it bridges that theory and practice gap that can exist without it. So, if that professor works directly with schools, their own knowledge and ability to affect change increases.

This holds true for all who are teachers of adults in education. Without a firsthand knowledge of what is happening, challenges that exist, current practices, and resources available, how can one be able to successfully help adult learners? If they are missing those aspects of application, then they are just teaching empty theories. Experiential learning is an important aspect of adult learning and being able to bring activities that mimic the realities that teachers or principals could face on the job are critical. The more a professor, department, or institution is connected to local schools, the more this benefits all parties.

Partnerships do not need to be limited to colleges and universities. Local business, industry and community are the perfect place for rich experiences to happen. There are opportunities for what are sometimes called senior work study programs. These are great programs where students who have the room in their schedules can spend time shadowing and working with designated businesses and industries in the community. While these offer valuable opportunities for some students, there are many students who do not get to participate in these opportunities. Beyond the lack of access to some seniors, what about creating access for other younger students?

What is the responsibility for local businesses, industries, and communities to invest back into their schools? Today there are fewer opportunities for students to learn about careers in schools. Challenging sets of standards exist that leave less room for electives. All standards are available to any stakeholder and offer a wonderful opportunity to forge partnerships. Common core standards for English language arts have a strong focus on nonfiction text, evidence from text, and bringing text from multiple disciplines into the nonfiction readings. Knowing this, many local businesses could find ways to engage with students and vice versa.

While Common Core Standards are not what they once were—intended to be standards for all states—most states that adopted them still use the standards either in their entirety or with a simple name change. It should also be noted that the creation of the standards began with a review that was led by commissioners of education, governors, corporate chief executive officers, and leaders in higher education. This inclusive process to develop these important standards should be mirrored in partnerships to apply them. Leaving all learning around these standards to a school level is a missed opportunity.

Where are local experts in this process? It is always nice when a school has the funds to take a field trip to a local museum, farm, or natural area. These experiences are all too rare and may not provide equitable access to all students. Students in more affluent districts and in areas with more local programs can have more experiences. So how can one leverage local resources to become a part of the school? Can one not find ways to bring experts into classrooms more often? Can one not find ways to help show students what is out there?

While these interactions would optimally be done in person, we know that technology can bridge this gap. Could a local expert not virtually join classes in multiple schools simultaneously thanks to available technology? If the pandemic has taught the educational world anything, it is that distance is not limited to physical space. Work and education can continue in person or remotely. Technology and a plan are great equalizing factors.

These partnerships do not have to be one directional. The more engaged a school is with the community, the more projects can exist and the more involved their students can be. Community service opportunities will present themselves. Ownership and pride throughout a community between schools and local entities benefit everyone involved. This cycle continues and grows as the expectations of service and partnership grow. Areas and examples mentioned before are just the surface of where partnerships can go and become. This level of applied learning can be invaluable to students.

To return to the focus and charge of this text, it is time to look at solutions once again on how to improve schools. This involves trying to find new ways to make improvements or new ways to look at the problems education faces. Local resources could offer support that may not have been previously considered. Nothing mentioned in this text is a magic bullet or a one-size-fits-all miracle cure. Anything mentioned in this book will need to be further explored, and thought will have to be given to how to implement or initiate a relationship or action. Some ideas in this chapter will be better options for some schools than others, but regardless of the idea and application, there is growth to be gained.

No one is naive enough to think that a local college or university could immediately take over the statistical analysis of all local schools. Similarly, doing research for innovative best practices in all local schools is also unrealistic. However, could a school district not identify a subset of struggling schools and partner with a professor or higher learning institution to build a foundation for beginning a process? Could a school with an outdated library or lacking a librarian not make a connection with one in town? It is not always the best approach to try to solve all problems at once. Moving in the right direction and getting started can be a good path.

Change takes time. Change also takes trying things that have not been tried or trying things in a unique way. Everyone should be able to identify opportunities to leverage resources that could benefit students, so now is the time to act on what one knows could help all students achieve more. Identify within one's locus of control a local resource that could help an area of need in a school. Find a way to make that relationship beneficial for both sides and begin to affect some positive change.

Chapter 6

Licensure and Assessment
A Path Forward

In the vane of school improvement, looking at the primary players is a reasonable place to begin. Teachers are the ones that have the most direct contact and greatest impact on students' education. It makes sense that the better prepared teachers are when they enter the profession and the better they are trained while in their positions, the more effectively they can instruct and positively impact student learning. When was the last time that a true audit and review of state and national licensure requirements and processes was completed?

Given the difficulty that states and districts are having filling teacher vacancies, changing licensure to become more stringent or to add requirements would not be a popular nor practical idea at this time. However, the goal here is to explore ways to improve schools. One path to improving schools is to improve the skills of the main stakeholder that affects student learning: the teacher. While most ideas in this text can be implemented right away, this chapter will be devoted to a more global idea that needs attention, even if it is outside the locust of control of most of this text's readers.

This text has already examined the varied paths available to enter education and the diverse adult learners this creates. The idea of examining licensure practices is not to create a common, one-size-fits-all set of teachers. It is time to review an archaic process that can be improved to improve education. The skillset needed for effectively teaching today's students is different than it was last year, let alone decades ago. Theories have been revised and created that help meet learners' needs. Tools and technologies are now available that revolutionize how educators can differentiate for student needs and design instructional experiences.

Licensure, while currently an ongoing process, should be revised to reflect a more continuous process. There should be tiers to this vital process. Licensure for a traditional path to a teaching certificate should begin with a requisite set of content and theory courses and knowledge. This would match what is available at current and typical colleges and universities. This is also what many current licensure requirements have. This set of skills and concepts would represent the base level of certification needed to enter a classroom job in education.

This would not represent a cost or burden to institutions of higher education, as this already comprises the vast majority of what education departments offer and specialize in. While this is in place already, everyone from state departments of education down to individual college departments should review these programs annually to make sure they are up to date with emerging theory, skills, and concepts. Updating programs, courses, and course outcomes is a necessary reflective practice. The mindset of being cutting-edge should be where education shifts to and lives.

While this base-level tier is a good start in preparing soon-to-be professionals for the world of education, it should be just the first step. The next step should be more specific and current. This step should include endorsements that go on the license. These endorsements can be what sets candidates for jobs apart. Endorsements can include many areas of focus and learning.

One example of a possible licensure endorsement could be becoming proficient in a specific learning management platform such as Google Apps for Education. Many schools and districts have adopted this or similar platforms to serve as learning management systems. Being able to learn about specific programs, through an accredited system so that it could be added onto a license, would add knowledge and value to perspective job candidates and could be added by current employees. While just one example, having mastery of skills, knowledge, or a technology and being able to attach it to a license is a way to better know our adult learners.

This simple second tier would save schools and districts time and money on training new employees if those new employees were able to gain important knowledge prior to being hired. Similarly, current employees can seek endorsements that meet school and district needs to have essential skills and knowledge. Having an endorsement system is a way to help standardize access to knowledge and skills. These endorsements would serve in place or alongside a resume or curriculum vita to allow a system of transparency with this knowledge and skills.

A system where offerings are available through multiple means could help with access and equity to these programs while expanding opportunities to engage. Leveraging online courses, continuing education credits, and other means previously discussed in this text could help to give more educators the skills they need to be successful given a school's preferred resources while also leveraging the licensure process as a continuing growth tool for educators. A necessary feature would be a level of oversight of the type of institution that offers the courses and ensuring that the objectives and outcomes are aligned to both the state and local institutions associated with the educators seeking an addition to their license.

This adult learning opportunity speaks directly to the partnerships mentioned in the local resource chapter. If states and districts can partner with higher education institutions regarding important initiatives, then courses, certificates and learning opportunities can be created to provide endorsements. Districts and schools can leverage these as needed to support employees with this learning. The possibilities of how this can be managed are exciting to think about. This can also focus learning opportunities for schools and districts to maximize these courses that would be created by designers familiar with adult learning best practices.

This would also create a system where undergraduate students can craft a license that is tailored to a district or state they wish to work for. This is a system that benefits all stakeholders. This is the type of system that strengthens local partnerships and better prepares learners to be successful in specific schools.

Imagine a new teacher walking into their first day of school already being proficient in the school's online-learning management system, standards, student intervention strategies, and primary curriculum resources. The learning curve for this type of teacher would be different than what is faced currently. Many of the barriers of learning new programs will be removed. Time can then be spent mentoring and coaching, as opposed to providing basic-needs systemic support.

This type of system also has value for current employees. Those seeking jobs at other schools or desiring promotions can have access to a transparent list of desired skills and sets of knowledge and the means and opportunities to gain them. This is a continuous, growth-based system that rewards ambition while eliminating certain barriers. This also helps to give employees direction in how they improve. Where educators now often renew licenses with what can be a random list of courses from varied institutions, this system could help to offer a more systemic approach.

Schools, districts, and states can also leverage a system like this one as new initiatives are introduced. If a specific strategy is going to be integral to improvement efforts at a school or more globally, an opportunity to leverage this into the continued-licensure process is a way to ensure that all educators have the requisite knowledge needed to support this new initiative. This also will help adult learners see the value by way of orientation in the learning if this additional layer of opportunity to connect learning to the license is enacted. This could prove valuable for new curriculum adoptions, technology programs, and other research-based best practices.

This creates a systemic approach with an aligned vision and purpose. Current licensure requirements are loose once someone is employed. Educators widen their knowledge gap through free choice in most current systems. Personal growth is important, yet, if it is done completely in isolation, this does little to advance the system. Narrowing the focus, giving some control back to the school to help with common knowledge and understanding is a way to bring staff into a unified place for meeting student needs. Having specific learning as a direction that the school needs to meet these challenges while tying it to licensure can help with school improvement.

Other industries in the world expect their employees to keep up with specific skills and learning or they become obsolete. This is a reasonable expectation and one that the field of education has been too loose with in the past. A tiered system benefits all stakeholders by allowing skillsets of educators to reflect the schools they already work for or desire to work for and a transparent way to know what is expected and needed from them. How states choose to quantify the tiers and requirements is beyond the scope of this text. However, looking at improving the current system is within the scope.

This endorsement concept is not new to education. Some states, districts, and organizations already employ variations of this. One example of this that stands out is how many states handle Advanced Placement courses. College Board has a strong system in place for preparing teachers as well as auditing course syllabi. They host a network of week-long courses meant to provide knowledge in each specific Advanced Placement course that is offered to students. These courses are offered on site and online for Advanced Placement teachers across the United States and even for teachers around the world.

While high school teachers who have a teaching license went through, what in many states, equates to a full bachelor's degree in their content area, College Board still offers an elevated level of learning around their rigorous Advanced Placement offerings. States have different requirements for being eligible to teach an Advanced Placement course. Many education institutions will require a teacher to first attend a week-long summer institute to help their chances of success with this teaching assignment. Some states require teachers to attend these periodically.

An Advanced Placement endorsement on a teaching license, for those states and organizations that use the system, is a wonderful way to both prepare a teacher and to know what skills a teacher possesses. Since teaching an Advanced Placement course is widely considered a prestigious appointment, knowing what teachers have successfully prepared to do so can be helpful when a high school is hiring someone. This helps to merge the idea of a license with a resume or curriculum vita. Many districts get creative with funding to pay for teachers to attend these valuable institutes. If a more universal system of learning and endorsement were to be created districts and states could similarly allocate funds to meet the most pressing needs of students and schools.

The ideas in this chapter are not new. Licenses are required for educators. Learning is tied to earning licenses and tied to maintaining a license. Yet, there exists an opportunity to both improve and standardize this process to benefit all stakeholders in education. If a system could be created to reward people who have specific knowledge and skills in a transparent manner that has a level of oversight, everyone could benefit. This type of system would further connect and network schools to higher education institutions and would allow for a better, more efficient system of improvement. Improving teachers and their access to growth is a pathway to improving schools.

Reforming licensure on a large scale for educators is an idea that needs to be explored but not one that will happen quickly nor uniformly across the United States. While the right reform could have a profound impact on education, getting even some state-level departments of education to review their practices is a good first step. A byproduct of the current processes in place for licensure is the reality of the diverse educational backgrounds of teachers. This variance represents a strength and a potential barrier to schools maximizing their human resources.

Time was spent earlier in this text laying a foundation regarding the concept of how the diverse skillsets that educators bring to their profession based on their previous degrees, previous jobs, and what they learned along their career journeys produces educators that each have a unique set of skills and experiences. The benefit of this for students is clear. Students get to experience and learn from diverse teachers with unique perspectives and talents. They get to benefit from teachers who took different courses, attended different universities, and had different paths to their career, thus allowing them to gain different knowledge from varied instructional techniques.

The positive aspects of this are shaded by the negative reality of how problematic it is to effectively differentiate learning for a group of diverse educators with little common background nor identical level of understanding on most topics. Even two teachers who graduate from the same university and program may have had different courses or professors, which could impact their level of knowledge or skillset. Yet is this not a self-created problem? Differentiation while embracing differences should be the norm in education and educating teachers. Convenience, ignorance to best practices of adult learning, and a system where bad habits in educating our educators have taken school improvement down a poor path.

Education is different from other fields in that, educational differences would not matter for a doctor or lawyer or other profession where standard exams determine mastery and readiness for employment and job opportunities. Education seems reluctant to engage in this practice relying on coursework to dictate mastery and readiness. When looking for opportunities to improve, it is often time to think creatively and look at what can be changed and improved to affect the desired outcome.

Licensure examinations exist for education. When looking at what each state requires, it is easy to see how disjointed the nation's education system is. Given the constant changes that some states make in their requirements, putting a comprehensive list of state exams for licensure in this text would prove to be obsolete by the time this is published. Instead, a brief overview of differences will be highlighted. For the reader, a quick internet search can yield current requirements, as can a visit to any state department of education website.

Some states do not require testing if the candidate has completed an approved degree program. Some states require testing on one or more of the following: content and subject areas, the ability to instructionally plan, understanding of pedagogy, understanding of reading, the ability to address diverse populations, and the list goes on. Some states create their own tests, others use tests from Praxis or companies like Pearson.

These requirements change often and again present gaps in knowing the knowledge and skills of our teachers. While this can be relatively effective for a teacher who plans to spend their entire career in one state, not everyone starts and ends their career in the same school, let alone state. There exist partnerships between states for direct reciprocity of licensure and others where additional testing is needed. The process of knowing what is required and how to be eligible to teach in other states is a tricky one to navigate in a field already facing teacher shortages. Any additional barrier is something that could and should be avoided when possible.

Testing is an effective method to gauging understanding. However, when requirements are so varied and have changed over time, what data does that testing provide as new learning and initiatives are introduced? States creating updated testing requirements is a way to help ensure new teachers have a specific knowledge base, but what about the current teachers who have not been assessed on their knowledge for decades? Furthermore, there have been countless hours devoted to learning at the school level and often little ability to effectively measure the mastery and implementation of the focus of that learning. This area, which is directly tied to school improvement, presents an opportunity for growth within education.

To continue being solution oriented, this presents an opportunity. While the past cannot change and gaps will exist, having a system moving forward to measure knowledge and catalog that knowledge would benefit all in education and help improve the function of schools through a more efficient and data-driven process of learning. Imagine a comprehensive and ever-growing set of skill and competencies assessments that could be taken by educators in a controlled environment. The applications of a system such as this could be powerful.

A designer of professional learning could use competency tests as a pretest to see where the learners currently are. If a system were in place where competencies were catalogued, then certain educators would not necessarily need to be assessed nor taught as their mastery would already be recorded. Those who demonstrate mastery could receive a different, personalized learning experience. Data could be used to group learners and the designer could provide a differentiated learning experience for their adult learners. Professional learning days for adults in schools would be revolutionized. Gone would be the days of one-size-fits-all experiences that meet the needs of a few but not the majority, and a data-informed method of improvement could be realized.

Combining assessments with the idea of endorsements on licenses along with a system and commitments to partnering with higher education for learning opportunities creates a continuum of assessing needs, providing supports, motivating learners, and measuring outcomes. For as much as those in education are expected to do this with young students, the expectations around learning for those same adults falls short for this type of process and best practice. What is good for some should be good for all. The blueprint for this model is achievable and simple.

This process would start with a clear mission and vision for the state, district, or school looking to change their practice and improve. This institution would then identify what priorities they value, what theories in education they subscribe to, what primary resources they want to be areas of focus, and what strategies they want teachers to utilize for the best interest of student learning. Most schools, districts, and states already know most or at least some of this, however, taking a step back and reflecting on this is always a good practice. This reflection, along with the mission and vision look vastly different between schools, districts, and states; however, a plan could be created at any of those levels and could help systemically inform one another.

Once a clear vision for the priorities is created, a means to and plan for how prioritized learning can be created is made available to educators and administrators. A plan to measure this learning would be an integral part of this process and a plan to measure the impact it has on students is equally important. In the next chapter, time will be spent examining how technology and some creative approaches to learning are making information and courses more accessible than ever and leveraging these opportunities will make ambitious plans for improvement easier than ever before.

The ultimate goal here would be a system of learning and assessment that is aligned to priorities and goals. There would still be opportunities for individualized learning needs, but systems need to consider the big picture and primary priorities while finding ways to have common practices and common understandings for the good of students. If a research-based strategy is deemed the best way to address a specific deficit in a school, then measurable, common learning for those who need it is something that schools or districts should be able to provide. Having a trackable system to catalog who has mastered this skill and who has not is a way to prioritize where support can be allocated.

This type of plan will require work and a desire to change. Consequently, it brings a level of transparency and accountability into practice. Again, imagine how powerful it could be to have new teachers coming straight out of college walking into a school already possessing the very skillset that the school is prioritizing for their student populate. Imagine a suite of assessments that a school or district could utilize to see where their staff knowledge is regarding an important theory in education. Imagine a plan to fill gaps of knowledge that is data driven and differentiated based on what the staff needs.

Replacing the poor practice of not leveraging learners' experiences with sounds andragogy in the framework of how learning takes place in districts and schools would be revolutionary. Student-centered learning based on mastery and data would be a dynamic step to help improve schools. Resources are spent every year by every school on improvement efforts yet needs still exist. Changing approaches to how educator knowledge is measured and how that data is used to inform instructional needs will improve the current state of adult education for teachers.

The most powerful benefit that any of these ideas would be the creation is a true system of learning. Public education in both the licensure and improvement domains has failed to create a systemic approach of common knowledge and learning that adheres to best practices of adult learners. The current model of having no accountability, no way to measure knowledge, and no way systemically to use data to help design learning experiences that meet learners where they are is not an effective or efficient approach. It is time to change practices to improve results.

Chapter 7

Technology and Online Learning
The Shrinking Educational Universe

This is an exciting time in the world of education to live in and be a part of. Within the last two decades, the education world began to shrink, and specifically, shrank for learners' benefit. There was once a time when educators factored ideas like "can I leave right after work and still make it to a night class?" If the answer was no, a course or degree was decided against or pushed off to a later date. While in-person education is still a great option for many learners, it is no longer the only option. Distance learning is not a new idea, yet even this area has changed, continues to change and changes for the better by providing increased access to more learners.

So, what is available for today's educator with respect to options for education? This starts with a look at online learning trends. There are a lot of statistics available that capture trends in online course participation and online degrees. The following data from Oregon paints a strong picture. According to the Higher Education Coordinating Commission, over the timeframe from 2008/2009 to 2018/2019, the following trends occurred with university students in Oregon. The number of students taking at least one online course increased 151 percent. The percentage of students taking no online courses decreased from 72.5 percent to 37.5percent.[1]

Using the same time period another interesting data point emerges. The percentage of students taking only online courses increased from 6.2 percent to 14.2 percent. Keep in mind this is data from just before the pandemic. It makes sense that the pandemic will move these types of numbers even higher. People are seeking opportunities to leverage distance learning to meet their needs and schedules while preserving their time. The number of people doing so is increasing and appears set to continue to increase.[2]

The 2020 version of the Online College Students Comprehensive Data on Demands and Preferences report reveals some interesting insight about students taking online courses. In 2020, 75 percent of students taking online courses were within 50 miles of their institution. Looking back at the idea of partnerships and local resources, leveraging local universities for educational opportunities continues to be an important idea despite the venue. When thinking about quality of online education, 78 percent of students said their experience was as good if not better online compared to face-to-face. If adult learners' needs are being met, online opportunities should be further leveraged.[3]

The structures and approach to revenue in higher education are changing. Undergraduate programs were once fully run as face-to-face options. A lengthy and careful admissions process would ideally lead to exactly 100 percent of the desired first-year class population. Next schools would have to pair attrition rates and factor in students desiring to transfer in from other institutions or two-year programs to keep upper grades enrollment optimized. These practices worked for decades and are still employed for face-to-face learning, but the addition of more online learning has changed operations and revenue models to help colleges.

Learners are not always looking to commit the time and finances to a full program. This is where technology and the shrunken world of education are doing some of its best work and further benefiting the learner. The rise of continuing education courses for nonmatriculating students as well as massive open online courses (MOOCs) and EdCamps are changing the game to bring learning to learners. In a way, these programs are offering the same access to knowledge that encyclopedias previously provided to prior generations, and all one needs is a laptop, smartphone, or tablet to unlock a world of learning opportunities.

"Continuing education" is a term that is often thrown around but rarely defined. Continuing education speaks to a broad category of certificates and stand-alone courses offered by colleges and universities. Most of these opportunities are designed for nonmatriculating students. Credits are earned based on the hours committed to the courses that are chosen. The typical metric for a continuing education unit, CEU, is ten hours of work, but this varies. This concept is not limited to the field of education. Many other professions have access to CEUs to help organize learning and educate adult learners.

While the idea of CEUs is not a free one, it is still shrinking the world and putting courses and certificates at the fingertips of education professionals. The beauty of this system is that these courses and even certificate programs can be quickly written, designed, and added to the choices of what a learner is looking to gain knowledge in. Courses about distance learning, synchronous and asynchronous learning, even teaching in a COVID-19 environment were available to learners who knew where to look for them. Educators looking for ways to grow personally, professionally, or based on job requirements have many options to do so through CEUs.

This type of system and access is not just a benefit for the learner. This brings a whole new revenue stream for colleges and universities. Good courses that create buzz online will attract learners. Good advertising by institutions can benefit everyone from designer to learner to institution. While the benefit of having someone commit to a degree and the costs that come with it are strong for an institution, having a plethora of low overhead offerings that participants pay for upfront, which can be run on simple learning-management platforms, offers great revenue potential for schools.

Continuing education is an easy revenue source that creates timely and needed learning options. Interested students benefit from the learning and they support an institution that gains a student and funds. Once an institution has desirable offerings in courses, they can leverage those ideas by creating more courses in line with these as well as create certificate program options comprised of multiple courses. Institutions now have learners looking to invest more into themselves and more money into that university or college. The system is a great benefit to all involved and gaining more popularity. Yet, there is still room to grow.

Colleges and universities should leverage these benefits, the credits, and certificates, to increase collaborations with local districts or schools to create custom learning opportunities. This is a fantastic way for partnerships to form, strengthen and mutually benefit each other as initiatives from districts can be used to help spark that extrinsic motivation of credits and what comes along with them for learners. This is not just done for the betterment of schools; the institution gets the tuition and has gained new and potential repeat customers. Institutions also gain field experience to learn of trends and needs, helping their growth.

If a school knows that it has an initiative or area of focus that requires design of learning experiences, having a willing partner is mutually beneficial. The institution can create and facilitate learning opportunities for the school or district. This puts learning in the hands of people with strong backgrounds with adult learning theory. Again, looking beyond financial benefits, the university is also gaining insight into current and emerging initiatives in various subjects and grade levels.

Massive online open courses, or MOOCs, are an idea that started in 2008. While credit to this idea is not agreed upon, MOOCs have been around for almost a decade and a half. The concept of MOOCs grew and got more popular in 2011. The idea of a MOOC is simple: it is to offer a free online course to anyone who wants to enroll. Many well-known and prestigious colleges and universities participate in and offer MOOCs, as do smaller institutions and companies. This concept is worldwide and can tackle learning to include college prep, basic training, career changes, or simply personal improvement.

MOOCs can be a vehicle to revolutionize changes within an industry. When innovative technologies emerge, a MOOC for a new and innovative concept can help teach a skill or important knowledge for an ambitious group of learners who want to stay relevant in the workforce. MOOCs can also serve as the primary platform for research. Imagine having a willing and large test population from which to gather data. There are many ways these far-reaching learning experiences can positively affect both the user and the creator.

In education, MOOCs are yet another way that technology and innovation are providing content and learning experiences for willing participants. Those in the field looking to gain new skills, sharpen existing skills, or explore innovative ideas can access and participate in MOOCs for free without the commitment of a degree program or even a set schedule. In the age of information sharing, MOOCs offer the ultimate platform to those wanting a risk-free option for learning. Some colleges and universities even allow work from MOOCs to be submitted for credit or research hours. This further increases the extrinsic motivation to participate in these learning experiences.

Specifically for teachers, a quick online search yields a wealth of options for types of MOOCs that currently exist with more of these classes becoming available. Popular and timely course areas available in these platforms include eLearning, twenty-first century schools and classrooms, blended learning, virtual instruction, social emotional learning, and Common Core. While this is only a small sample of what is available, these are specific topics that are vital for educators in today's classrooms that are often only glazed over in a typical university course or are only touched on in a limited fashion during staff development.

The important part to focus on is not only the ease of access and lack of cost, but also the ability for the creators to design learning experiences that fit a current need in society. When looking through the lens of what is really important in education today, one must remember that there are many veteran educators who received their degree decades ago and had a course and program focused on ideas and strategies that are less relevant today than when they were first taught. Gone are the days of the idea that a quiet classroom is a sign of learning, and gone are the days of nice, neat rows of desks that help keep students in an orderly, alphabetical fashion.

MOOCs can level the playing field for teachers of any age and experience level. Being able to access new and timely information that fits today's world is a game changer for not just the teacher but for the whole school community. Access to information is a strength of today. Making that information available to people for free is the best look at where society is and where it can go. Do enough schools and districts promote these valuable opportunities? How can a school or district maximize the visibility and knowledge of what is out there and how it can impact instruction and overall improvement?

This is where supervisors, schools, and districts need to keep up with the times. If these options are available to teachers, it is the responsibility of supervisors, schools, and districts to bring that information to their educators. It is their responsibility to help find MOOCs or other courses that fill a need with that school, its population, and data-driven goals and initiatives. Many schools require teachers to have personal or professional growth plans to be updated yearly or periodically. Embedding an expectation to participate in learning, free or otherwise, is reasonable and beneficial. Leveraging specific MOOCs can only benefit all parties involved.

Sticking with the theme of how technology is shrinking the world and making education accessible to more, one needs to look at the idea of an EdCamp. EdCamps have a less mysterious origin as compared to MOOCs. EdCamps were started by a group of educators after they attended a BarCamp Philly in 2009. The concept and rules behind a BarCamp inspired a group of attending teachers to change how learning occurred in education. The ideas of how an EdCamp, BarCamp, or what is known as an unconference are run and are participated in, run contrary to most typical learning experiences that are created for teachers in a school environment.[4]

Next will be a look at some of the differences between a typical learning experience that teachers are subjected to compared to an EdCamp, BarCamp, or unconference-type setting. Typical professional learning has a top-down, driven agenda and set of goals. An EdCamp is attendee driven. This first difference highlights how typical learning experiences may not follow principles of adult learning while the design of an EdCamp can account for adult learners' needs. Unconferences use the idea that anyone can claim a timeslot and offer their expertise on a topic. This differentiates itself from a typical learning experience for teachers.

While the rules of EdCamps mirror those of BarCamps, the primary ones to focus on for the purposes of an adult learner in the field of education are who presents and who is given that opportunity. This text focused earlier on the importance of the role that experience plays in adult learning. Look how naturally that fits with the idea that anyone who wants to offer their expertise is invited to participate and lead a session. Experience is valued, celebrated, and recognized with this format. Professionals are given a voice and a platform to share. Sadly, this is not the norm of most learning experiences within current educational institutions.

Professional learning days or events within a school are often dictated by a top-down approach. Teachers serve as receivers of information through what may be a passive or active approach, but they are still being taught. These events are facilitated by an administrator, visitor from a district office, or at times a teacher leader. However, the dynamic is not one that gives ownership to the participants. If sound adult learning theory teaches anything, it is the importance of the learner's experience and how critical this is to the success of a learning event. The inherent design of an EdCamp or unconference puts this experience where it needs to be: front and center.

Circling back to the andragogical process model and general assumptions of adult learners, it was clear the importance of mutual goal setting and mutual planning play for adult learners. EdCamps exemplify this by giving control to participants who can simultaneously be the designers, facilitators, and learners. This further highlights the assumption of the self-concept. Choice for how participants interact, choice in content, and choice in sharing knowledge are all powerful for adult learners.

Another positive aspect of an EdCamp is that it was designed to be free. While there can be instances that costs for venues or supplies can exist and sponsors are not always available, cost is not meant to allow anyone to profit. However, adhering to the idea of free is something that does not always happen. This author has personally seen events advertised as EdCamps with the unconference model that still have an entry fee with no transparency in why there is a cost. While these are the exception and not the rule, it is still noteworthy to mention that even with best intentions on a model and philosophy, there are still some who can try to profit when this clearly goes against the EdCamp philosophy.

It is encouraging that some schools and districts have dabbled in the concept of EdCamps and unconferences. The real question is, why haven't more? This speaks to an underlying hypocrisy in current educational institutions. Districts and leadership expect innovation out of their teachers, yet fail to employ best practices for adult learners when they are given opportunities. Again, the question of why schools are not improving, why instruction is not changing, and why students are not growing often has those individuals looking to fix the problem by looking in the wrong place.

The point of bringing up the shrinking world is to show a ray of hope. Educators have access to so many paths to learn new skills and to sharpen existing tools. Educators can access colleges and universities that were geographically impossible to access before recently. Online courses and degrees are at one's fingertips, and the benefits will be felt by many when educators invest in that type of learning. Continuing education is another way for educators to access more targeted concepts without a long-term or heavy financial commitment. The benefits gained are great, and the time and cost are now more manageable. Readiness is clearly supported.

While traditional courses, degrees, and credits are more comfortable for some learners, the idea of shared learning and free education is picking up steam. Access for educators to take full advantage of MOOCs is readily available, so long as they know that these opportunities exist and are even encouraged to participate. It is a collective responsibility to share and advertise these experiences. These should not be exclusive learning events; they were designed with the opposite in mind. However, some districts and schools fail to be knowledgeable or fail to promote experiences outside of their direct control and do so to the detriment of their stakeholders.

EdCamps are easily available and accessible as they can take place virtually or in a face-to-face environment. They do not necessarily require a learning management platform and can begin once someone has something to share. This type of model of a learner-centered experience where the event is driven by the participants, is a model in line with best practices of adult learning theory. While something like this does not need to be the format of every learning experience at a school, taking best adult learning practices into design should be a mandatory exercise for those working to design learning experiences.

Where does one go from here? The start should always focus on education and awareness. Learning experiences should follow best practices for adult learners. New, semi-new, or simply improved venues for learning opportunities need to be brought to every educator's attention. One cannot begin to improve and change if they continue to do the same things repeatedly. Discrete, one-size learning experiences will not best meet the needs of all teachers and are far from best practice. Making better efforts to both design and share awareness and access with learners is a good forward step.

While experience was highlighted in this chapter as a crucial factor in adult learning, one cannot underestimate the idea of readiness. The learner being ready to experience and take on a concept, skill, or strategy is crucial for adult learners. When the only learning or staff development a teacher receives is something on a fixed school year calendar and has preset objectives, how ready can any participant be? But when a course, degree program, or credit option can be enrolled in at any point or a continuing education class, or MOOC is self-paced or an easily accessible EdCamp is available, readiness can be met for the adult learner.

Just because a district or school deems an initiative to be important does not mean that an adult is ready to receive it. This is not defiance; this is simply how adults are wired to receive information. Instead of continuing with the "old" habits of how they have tried to make education work in the past for adult learners, one needs to rethink how to approach improvement through learning. This problem is not one without a solution, it is one that needs an intentional change in approach to help ensure that adults' needs are a part of the design. Innovative practices and venues should be considered instead of a stagnant approach. It is everyone's responsibility to do better.

The need to know, self-concept and orientation to learn are intentionally addressed with the examples in this section. Design and access are what make these assumptions a focus for adult learners. It would take a learner seeing a need and wanting to address it to enroll in an online course, MOOC, or EdCamp. The choices available in types of learning experiences that these options represent help with self-concept and an adult's need for choice and direction. Finally, the choice to seek one of these learning experiences shows a problem was identified to be addressed to meet orientation. More intentionality with efforts can help better meet school's needs.

The focus to change and improve should be solution oriented. Within one's locus of control, what can one do to help support the school, district, or institution? Can one bring examples of online learning to their leadership? One may know of a university that is willing to partner and create a CEU course for colleagues. Perhaps one knows of powerful CEU courses already created, or interesting and relevant MOOCs, or EdCamps. Sharing knowledge and bringing information to those who make decisions is a small but necessary step. These efforts might start an innovative approach in how adult learning is leveraged.

NOTES

1. Lynn Wallis, "Growth in Distance Learning Outpaces Total Enrollment Growth," State of Oregon Employment Department, 2020.
2. Wallis, "Growth in Distance Learning Outpaces Total Enrollment Growth," 2020.
3. A. J. Magda et al., *Online College Students 2020 Comprehensive Data on Demands and Preferences*, Louisville, KY: Wiley Education, 2020.
4. Mary Beth Hertz, "Introduction to EdCamp: A New Conference Model Built on Collaboration." *Edutopia* (blog), September 29, 2010.

Chapter 8

Climate

A Broad and Vital Area of Focus

Where one learns is an important element of how well they learn. Climate, while a broad concept with regard to adult education, can begin with how people often interpret it: the physical space in which someone engages in learning. Most everyone has learned the hard way, just as parents and teachers warned, that on the couch or in front of the television is not an optimal venue for the best learning or studying to occur. When one looks at more recent times and experiences, some found that learning online is a productive and empowering venue while others found it a struggle to replicate the proximity and formality of in-person learning.

While climate is more than physical space and its attributes, it is important not to overlook these, as they are impactful. Everything from the color of the room, the softness of chairs, the layout of furniture, and temperature are important and can affect learning. The proximity to restrooms and availability of food and beverages are also crucial factors to consider. The ability for learners to see and hear is vital. The temperature of the room is important because if someone is uncomfortable, this may hinder their ability to focus on learning. So, while climate is a broad concept, one must account for the basic interpretation first.

While some of these facets fall outside of the immediate control of an instructional designer or even a building leader, something as simple as the color of a room is an important consideration. Research has determined that while pale colors are found to be calming and relaxing, vivid colors contributed to much higher reading scores in university students. So, taking a solution-oriented approach, going outside of a traditional color palette for a school, especially in a space used for adult learning, should be considered. Furthermore, inexpensive LED colored lights could help invigorate a space where learning is meant to occur on specific days for adults.[1]

Convenience dictates that a space such as a school cafeteria is often a venue for adult learning in a school setting. Are student lunch tables comfortable for adults? Is that type of space optimal for grouping? Was a space like that designed for adults, let alone does it provide easy visual and physical access to resources and materials? While the idea of climate goes well beyond the aforementioned physical traits, it is time to rethink where learning events occur, so the location is intentional to maximize what is controllable.

Climate does go well beyond the physical attributes of a learning space, especially when the learning is designed for adult learners. There need to be some prominent features of climate to help adults better engage and feel comfortable learning. These elements include, but are not limited to, a trusting environment, respectful environment, and a supportive environment. These elements seek to reach the whole learner. Building trust, fostering respect, and providing support are all within the locus of control of the designer or facilitator.

A trusting environment is incredibly important for learning experiences with adults to be successful. As mentioned, the existence of a diverse population of educators is a blessing and a curse. Recognizing that this diversity gives a wealth of tools for students to experience and learn from is one of the great benefits. Recognizing that this diversity also leaves gaps in knowledge and skills that ultimately will need to be identified, addressed, and monitored is an important job of any educational institution. Knowing that these gaps are not the fault of the educators must be reinforced. This can support having a climate of trust that supersedes a climate focusing on differences being deficits.

Unfortunately, the word transparency is often met with skepticism, yet it is an important word to focus on. Transparency of expectations, transparency of areas of focus and transparency of supports available are all ways to help build a trusting environment within a climate of learning. A professional in any field, let alone education, should never have to guess what the expectations of their job are. If those expectations include, as they should, being a continual learner and having some or much of that learning focus on areas that will benefit the larger community, then everyone should be aware and regularly reminded of that expectation.

Transparency in educational goals and areas of focus within a department, staff or system could and should align with larger goals of the department, staff, or system. If this is not the case and alignment is not intentional, then once again there is the creation of new gaps in learning and skills or further broadening of existing gaps. How can one systematically improve without alignment? How can one be intentional and aligned without a proactive plan? Educators can relate to but should not have to relate to accreditation and other arbitrary timelines being the driver of improvement efforts. Transparency directly connects to a climate of trust.

Accreditation is a reality for many, if not most schools and educational institutions. It is an important mechanism and way of having checks and balances in place. However, it should not be the sole driver of how a school operates. It should be a way to measure how a school operates. If accreditation is the driver of change and improvement, then a school cannot be proactive with its own needs and direction. A proactive school can have a level of direction, planning and, thus, transparency that a school or institution that is working to solely pass an accreditation visit could never have. Proactivity and responsiveness should be the mindset of all efforts to improve.

The purpose of this chapter nor this text are not to vilify accreditation. It is quite the opposite. Processes of reflection, outside support, and partnerships are all best practices in education and other industries. Accreditation is a respected process that offers value to all institutions who participate. The example used above is one to refocus the need for continual growth cycles and processes outside of an accreditation visit or cycle. Many good practices can turn into a crutch or distract from their intended purpose if those in charge are not thinking globally nor not being proactive. The processes associated with growth should help and not hinder respect and trust.

Respect in the form of a two-way respectful culture between learner and designer of learning and learner and facilitator of learning is necessary to have a healthy system. Respect, like many other concepts, is a broad idea. An example of how the facilitator can demonstrate respect is being prepared for a learning experience. Respect can also be the learner coming prepared to learn during a learning experience. Respect is tied strongly to transparency and a proactive approach to education. Respect is also honoring, recognizing, and planning for the diverse set of learners that exist in a staff.

Respect also provides opportunities that meet the needs of everyone. Having space, access, time, and support for learning all fall under the broad category of respect. How can respect exist if one is not providing people with the resources and support? They need to meet the institution's vision of improvement. Being respectful of one's staff and learners means providing them with every opportunity to be successful. This means knowing their backgrounds, strengths, and weaknesses and helping to meet goals and milestones while also keeping them aware of their progress and next steps. This clearly connects to andragogy assumptions.

While addressing respect, one begins to address support. Ideas in climate and fostering relationships are interconnected. All too often one loses best practices that were employed with younger learners when it is time to work with adults. Teachers are respectful to the young students, they work hard to build trusting relationships with their young learners, and they look to offer them the support they need to be successful. Teachers use the best practices of giving them clear objectives during classes. They provide them with a syllabus, which gives an unmatched level of transparency for their own learning.

Yet too often a predetermined professional learning day is done to adult learners. Someone else determines what will be learned and why it will be learned. This may or may not be shared with the learners before a learning event happens. What someone knows are good practices gets forgotten, and this can happen for many reasons. Regardless of the reasons, it is the pattern that needs to change. This is the pattern that can change with a renewed and intentional focus on climate. Trust, respect, and support through a transparent, proactive vision are the keys to changing how effective learning can and will be realized in a school.

Now that there is a foundation, one needs to look at how this could be successfully implemented in a department, school, or system. While all three venues are different given the size each represents, looking at a school or institution is a fair middle ground to start the conversation. This look will include all aspects of climate as previously mentioned and focus on areas that can and should be changed and made a priority. The real question being asked is, what can one do to create a climate of learning for adults at a school that is comfortable and productive?

This conversation begins with the basic aspects of a climate. What physical space is provided for educators so that they can learn? Looking at most typical schools in the United States, there exist teacher lounges or planning spaces. These spaces typically serve two purposes. They are designed to have refrigerators and printers/copy machines. This creates an atmosphere of working and planning as well as eating and socializing. These are crucial functions. However, the desired focus for this discussion is on learning. Looking to create a physical space that is conducive to adults learning to systematically improve teacher knowledge and skills should be the ultimate focus.

Thinking about adult learners and what they would need physically in a space to help maximize their learning; the setup, color, and temperature of the room would have to be considered. A learning space that has both individual and collaborative seating environments would be beneficial for adults as it gives them a choice in how to best engage in learning. Any choice is important to adult learners. Furthermore, the ability to control the temperature is important for the comfort of adult learners. Access to computers is necessary, but since most teachers now have school provided technology, access to electrical outlets and Wi-Fi should be the new focus.

Having a collaborative environment that is comfortable and allows for choice in how one works and how one collaborates is a good start. School-specific curricular resources should be available in this space. Next is the need for targeted resources. Any journals that the school has membership with should be available here. Texts of aligned theories and practices should be available in hard copy. There should also be a mechanism to have support for online and digital resources. This should include access to the information specialist/librarian and educational technologist who should support the learning of both the students and teachers.

The ideas suggested above are not costly. However, the ideas above are creating an environment and climate that prioritizes a focus on adult learning. Would taking one copy room and transforming the space into a dedicated learning space for professionals have any negative impact on a school spatially, functionally, or financially? Giving professionals respect and the opportunity to foster growth is something every learning institution should be elevating as a higher priority. Developing human resources and giving them the space and support needed is a cultural shift that schools and leaders should value. If there is not an extra room, then a corner in the library or an empty office will suffice.

Imagine this new space. It is comfortable, has choice-based seating, access to Wi-Fi, power supplies, as well as physical and digital professional resources. Adding white boards, digital or old fashioned, gives individuals or groups space to record thinking, and a large screen to view videos of best practice gives more tools with which to learn and grow while doing so in a focused manner. There could be a dedicated board or wall for school goals, mission, vision, and common strategies and expectations. This space could serve as an epicenter of transparency and professionalism for the school.

Leadership expects teachers to post goals and objectives. They expect teachers to have a welcoming environment for their students. They expect teachers to display student work, have anchor charts, and employ best practices. Making a small shift in prioritization and intentionality with a work room, corner of the library, or other dedicated space allows for and begins the process of a culture of trust, respect, and support regarding the expectations of professional improvement. This shift or change in one space of the school where learning is the focus for teachers will have a positive impact in their growth and ultimately all students.

The "do as we say and not as we do" mentality can be erased in a workspace such as the one being described. School objectives will be posted and visible, modeling the same expectation given to teachers. Data will be available in hard copy as well as digitally so that every teacher can take ownership over every student. Anchor charts to model chosen data-analysis protocols will be posted. Exemplars of best practices will be on display. This can be a place where professionals can watch videos of lessons and hold discussions. This learning space for teachers will have everything a good learning space for any age should have.

Looking at how schools are commonly arranged, there are cultures or climates of isolation. Elementary schools typically have teams formed by grade levels. Grade level classrooms are close to each other. Planning and collaboration are accomplished together since they are teaching the same standards and grade-level subjects. But there is still a habit of grade level or team level isolation. This is the product of proximity and job-like commonality. While this is a positive pairing for collaboration, work and planning are often accomplished in one of their classrooms due to convenience. A dedicated space for learning will change the climate and mindset.

Middle schools are often similar yet have some distinct differences. Grade-level teams are often how buildings are arranged. Classrooms are set up so that a hallway or pod will consist of core subjects for a given grade level. This cuts down on passing time, which reduces discipline issues between classes. This represents intentionality with design while putting teachers who share students in proximity with each other and allows for collaboration and planning. Again, this is often accomplished with teams meeting in one classroom and working to plan. This further highlights the benefit and need of a dedicated learning space for adults.

In both prior examples, having teachers who share students located in close proximity to each other seems ideal. However, are these the only teachers that work with these students? Students take more than just core classes, and these other teachers that include, but are not limited to special education, gifted education, and electives, all can have a positive impact on the whole child yet can be physically distanced from grade-level collaboration opportunities. A shared, neutral space will improve culture by valuing all roles.

High schools have a unique design compared to elementary and middle schools. At smaller high schools, many teachers are often the only person or one of the few people teaching a particular course. Teachers tend to work in isolation and focus on their own courses and stay within their areas of expertise. Collaboration still happens but with more choice for students within their schedules. Teachers share fewer common students, and as a result, fewer natural collaborative partnerships based on courses or shared learners are leveraged. There is collaboration with common courses, common subjects, and common students, but again, natural fits are not always abundant or available.

One notable exception to this is the twenty-first-century school design. This design usually requires a new building to be constructed or a major renovation. This building is specially designed and built in a neighborhood concept. There are no permanent walls in these neighborhoods, and a collaborative space for learning is created. Beyond the lack of separation with students, the teachers also share collaborative space, and the expectation is for collaboration. This type of building and concept is the exception and not the norm. Yet, twenty-first-century schools are an intriguing design regarding having space to collaborate and focus on students and learning for adults.

Isolation, or working in silos, causes teachers to focus on their work and their learning. They plan in their own rooms and may not collaborate much or at all. Setting a climate and culture of shared learning, a shared learning space, and a functional learning space is crucial for all levels of schools. This ensures support and benefits climate. The space should clearly show expectations, offers the needed resources and support, as well as incorporates trust and respect as a step to empower professionals to come together and join into a situation where learning is accessible and an expectation for everyone.

What is more respectful than putting forth an effort to create an environment and climate to realize the learning that is required for a staff to move forward? When importance is paired with action instead of just words, people take notice. If a learning space is created and resources are provided to support systemic learning, a barrier has been eliminated. Equally important is creating a climate that will change a culture within a school. These types of solutions are not costly but take an intentional effort and commitment to establish. However, showing a staff that learning is a focus will be a positive step toward changing a climate and culture.

The goal of changing the climate is to get to where learning becomes part of school culture. More importantly, learning is something that the professionals in the building understand their need to know and are ready for whatever transparent and clear objectives the school, district, or organization have. This then becomes a continual process, not something that occurs in discrete learning events on professional development days. If this cultural shift happens, having the climate to include a functional space makes this practice sustainable and growth oriented for the staff and something that will in turn positively impact all stakeholders.

The concept of a university is a relevant comparison here. In a university, your tenured professors are all engaged in regular research. However, their goals for what they want to research and publish are not often aligned with the university. The professors work in silos, work on their own passions and projects, and may give little back to the local institutional community. Their research is valuable to the overall community of their field but not necessarily to the local community. In a school, the local community needs to be the focus. These silos that mirror a university do not benefit the most important stakeholder, the students.

Time was spent early in this book looking at the assumptions of adult learners. Time was also spent thinking about inducing some of these same assumptions because adult learners are often subject to learning that is mandated. The cultural shift explained in this chapter began with looking at all aspects of climate. This intentionality works to change the adult learner's perspective to know and value the importance of improvement. This is possible by the intentionality and dedication of leaders, designers, and facilitators to do their part.

Change is not easy, and change takes time. Simply creating a room and dressing it up a bit will not affect the desired change one wants and needs to transform schools. However, what if all leadership team meetings that focus on school improvement and school goals took place in this learning room? What if administrator and teacher meetings about classroom visits and observations took place in this room? The room already has resources related to school initiatives. The purpose of the space would be defined by improvement and learning. A consistent, transparent message is shared, while resources for support are easily accessible.

This space could serve as a designated research and learning area regarding professional growth plans. It could be where collaboration occurs with peers for instructional rounds. Having a place where the expectation is improvement separates the routines of grading and holding operational focused meetings from the work of learning and growing. For those who got their best studying in college done at the library or a dedicated space, this room would serve that same purpose and have a similar cognitive effect for the learner.

The purpose of this text is change and improvement. Promising ideas do not have to be completely revolutionary nor costly. The ideas in this text are meant to be ones that can be accomplished with an open mind and renewed focus. Being solution oriented, where can one begin? One can look at the physical spaces that are available and identify what is possible and what improvements are needed. One could shift the use of space and make a dedicated learning space and provide the necessary resources to it. One can schedule events, conferences, learning, focused meetings, and research in this space to give it purpose.

NOTE

1. Al-Ayash et al., "The Influence of Color on Student Emotion, Heart Rate, and Performance in Learning Environments," 197, 204–5.

Chapter 9

The Educator

A great deal of this text has been devoted to potential issues in education that if addressed could improve schools and academics for students. Teachers have been in the forefront of many of these topics, issues, and solutions. However, the teachers themselves have not been directly addressed and should be. As previously highlighted, teachers are the single most impactful element when it comes to the success of students in schools. Teachers are the ones with students all day. They are the ones who carry out a school's mission and vision and are central to all hopes of having the type of success in a school, district, or institution that one strives for.

This is the right time to examine how teachers feel in education and how a plan for their job satisfaction, health, and well-being are vital pieces for any chance to have the success being sought. This will not be a look at salaries and monetary compensation. Despite an attempt at being solution oriented, the extreme variances in salary based on schools, districts, states, and institutions creates a problem that cannot be easily fixed at the level of many of those reading this text. Excluding salary and compensation is not to say that all educators are fairly paid for all that they do. This is simply not something this text will take the time to try to rectify.

Where does the state of teacher satisfaction stand today? The logical place to start is looking at attrition rates. Stability has been difficult to maintain in schools as evidenced by high rates of teachers leaving their positions and even the profession. Over the past decade the annual turnover rate for teachers has averaged close to 8 percent. More troubling than this is how Title I–funded schools have averaged more than a 16 percent turnover rate during the same time period. The schools that need the best and most dedicated teachers are losing them at twice the rate of the national average. To put these numbers in perspective, Finland, Ontario, and Singapore, who are all considered high-performing places, average attrition rates between 3 and 4 percent annually.[1]

Teacher satisfaction is at an all-time low. Eighty-five percent of teachers feel that working conditions and school climate need more attention and need to be examined. The percentage of teachers who are very satisfied with their jobs declined over the period from 2012 to 2022 from 39 percent to 12 percent. This sharp decline represents the need for an urgent call to action. Those who are outside the world of education who see teachers as workers gifted with a summer off are out of touch with the realities and stressors that working with students, parents, politics, and the larger system of education represents.[2]

How do teachers really feel? In adult learning theory, as highlighted in the last chapter, respect is a crucial element of the climate and environment. Building a respectful and trusting environment is a part of the fabric for a successful experience for adult learners. A recent survey found that only 46 percent of teachers feel that the general public respects their profession. Ten years prior, that figure was at 77 percent. This significant decline has left more than half of educators feeling undervalued and not appreciated. How can educators perform at their best when they do not feel respected and appreciated at work?[3]

Not feeling respected by the community is a negative perception that comes to educators from outside of their immediate work environment. There are also factors within the environment that adversely affect educators. If employees face mental-health-related issues or well-being challenges at work, which can include anxiety, burnout, depression, or distress, their chances of reporting negative outcomes at work increase. Educators exhibiting any of these characteristics are four times more likely to say they will leave; three times more likely to report low job satisfaction, and two times more likely to report low engagement at work.[4]

The same characteristics also lead to a three-times-more-likely chance of experiencing toxic workplace behavior. This toxic environment may be the cause of peers, their supervisor, or a combination of the two. The important takeaway to realize with the idea of toxic behavior is that it is by far the greatest predictor of negative workplace outcomes. If a toxic environment were to be eliminated, the impact that could have on positive workplace outcomes is far greater than an inclusive work environment.

The existence of and focus on an inclusive work environment is important. This is the foundation of a respectful, trusting, and safe working environment. However, it was highlighted here because much attention is currently being paid to inclusivity, yet less is being paid to address toxic environments despite the greater impact addressing it could have. Yes, they appear to be related and have some overlap; however, if they are at times classified differently, then some different attention must be paid. Continuing the focus on inclusivity while adding a renewed focus on eliminating a toxic workplace should be a focus of schools and districts.[5]

The idea of a toxic workplace and teachers feeling a lack of respect are further impacted by a polarized political climate in the United States. Schools should be institutions that are nonpartisan and sheltered from the current toxic mindset that has become the norm within all levels and both sides of the current political landscape. Educators are being used as pawns for political agendas on both sides of the political aisle. The position this often puts teachers in can take them away from their own beliefs and become an added stressor that is exacerbated by fear of persecution and reprisal.

The incursion of politics into everything from curricula, courses offered, and day-to-day operations of schools takes away local control and makes the educator even more powerless over their place within a school. While this text cannot solve this problem, and there sadly does not seem to be a solution on the immediate horizon, recognizing this issue as a problem for the health and well-being of some educators is a key step. Districts and state boards of education stepping in to help shield schools from this unhealthy stressor is the next step. There should be a strong line drawn between education and politics and reestablishing that separation is necessary to help protect the mental health and well-being of educators for the best interest of the students they serve.

How does one define wellness? This is a broad category, especially in education. Wellness can focus on physical health. The global pandemic showed the world the importance of health, hygiene, and awareness. Wellness also focuses on mental health. For this understanding and a potential impact on improving schools, the mental side is where the majority of this text's focus will be. Mental wellness is a topic that is garnering more attention yet one that is not garnering enough. Schools have a focus on and a wealth of resources to help tend to students' mental health and well-being. Is there a single school or district where equal attention is being paid to the adults in the building? Is this lack of focus having an adverse effect on school performance?

Well-being is one of the top factors driving both teachers and administrators to leave the field of education. In recent surveys, well-being was stated as a factor in close to one-third of responses as a reason for wanting to leave. This is a substantial number that should garner the attention that it deserves. When comparing the factors for wanting to leave education, there are differences in the reasons given by teachers and administrators; however, the one factor that had similar rank and quantity was well-being.[6]

In a day and age when social and emotional learning and wellness is at the forefront of thought in the world of education, why is more attention not paid to the social emotional wellness of teachers? There is a clear connection to the impact that social and emotional learning (SEL) has in proper development of students and academic achievement. SEL is not limited to young students, yet it is often treated as being limited to these students. SEL, as described by CASEL, is the process through which adults and young students engage in self-awareness, self-management, social awareness, relationship skills, and responsible decision making. Those competencies are the foundation of SEL and are how evidence-based programs are designed.[7]

Many schools, districts, and organizations are currently implementing specific SEL programs for students. COVID-19 took time away from students to engage with peers and develop much needed social skills and interactions. The world of education is still catching up to the damage that this has done to many young learners who have lost years of development due to remote learning. Technology is changing how people interact and develop relationships. Adopting and implementing best practices in SEL, or even a specific program to address this, is a popular and needed direction that many schools, districts, and institutions are engaging in or exploring.

While addressing the most important stakeholders in education, the students, is not only the most direct but also the correct path to take in this process, why is more attention not being paid to the adult? What is being done to help ensure that adults feel heard, feel safe, feel respected, and feel like they are working in a healthy climate? Sadly, there are varying answers to this question and even on the better end of what is happening, those exemplars are not the reality in most places in education.

This text has strived to be solution oriented. Therefore, if teachers are not satisfied with their jobs, do not feel respected, and are struggling in their workplace, what can be done? Below is a start to an outline of possible steps that schools can take. Some of these may be in place already, but if enough of these were already in place, this would be a different conversation and this chapter might not be needed in a school improvement text. A combination of resources, structures, and programs should be a good start to address teachers' needs in educational institutions.

Community and colleagues play a leading role in teacher retention. The importance of how an educator feels about a connection to their workplace, their colleagues, and community should not be overlooked in the mission, vision, and improvement plan of an educational institution. How many schools include an intentional focus on putting steps in place to both improve and maintain the feeling of community and the opportunities necessary to build relationships amongst staff members? If eliminating a toxic environment can improve workplace outcomes and community and collegiality can help with retention, this should be a high priority.

How difficult would it be for building or district leaders to create monthly or regular opportunities to strengthen the community? This could be as simple as having standing social events outside of the hours of the workday once a month. This could include turning a teacher's lounge back into an actual teacher's lounge. Remove the copy machines and focus the space on a place for teachers to socialize and build on their relationships with one another. Time and space are both valuable assets in education and any industry; however, the positive impact they can have on a community should be deeply explored.

Questions that school leaders should regularly reflect on may include ideas around, how does the staff get along with each other? What opportunities are created for staff members to spend meaningful time with one another beyond doing their job requirements? When was the last time a school improvement initiative included a specific goal or action around the idea of community or collegiality? When was the last time any asset was allocated to the staff's health and well-being?

Intentionality is important in any improvement effort. Hoping that staff are happy in a toxic-free environment is not a pathway to a high-functioning educational institution. There needs to be a plan. Attrition rates are around 8 percent, which equates to approximately 1 in 12 staff members leaving each year. Building relationships and continuing to foster an opportunity for a strong and functional community would need to be a continual process. Regular engagements with opportunities for staff members to build their relationships and support networks are vital.

Any functional plan should also include support for new and veteran teachers alike. Support can ease stress and anxiety. Mentor programs should be in place and should also be regularly audited for their viability and impact. Having a mentor program is only the first step. Does the program have the proper mentors in place? Have those mentors been trained and given support for the work they do? Are mentors versed in adult learning theory? Is time an asset given to mentors to properly support their mentees?

Companies in industry have robust human resource departments. This includes support for mental health and well-being. Do all educators and teachers have the same access to this much needed level of support? As mentioned previously, there is a renewed focus on this level of support for students, as there should be. Students can have access to counselors, psychologists, mentors, and other professionals to help them navigate the challenges that school presents. Sixty-eight percent of schools employ a mental health professional while 51 percent employ an external professional to support students.[8]

How many schools and districts have dedicated professionals available to teachers? This author was unable to find any meaningful data on this topic. Despite the evidence of the importance of staff mental health and well-being, staffing to combat this appears to be minimal to nonexistent. Since positions are not necessarily allocated for this level of adult support and the absence of human resource departments in the mold of industry companies often do not exist in education, more of this responsibility falls on school and district level leaders.

The Center for Disease Control (CDC) recommends gathering data on the physical and nutritional needs of employees, administrative support in employee wellness and having a robust plan for eating, and physical programs for all employees. This comprehensive approach to wellness supports the physical and emotional well-being of employees and should be a part of all school improvement initiatives. The CDC cites that such programs can decrease absenteeism, health care costs, and improve retention and productivity.[9]

Due to the structures of schools and their inherent focus on students, the role of leadership in changing the culture and adding a focus of adult well-being is crucial. Structures and processes are important to affecting meaningful change. As mentioned before, time is a valuable asset that can be leveraged in many ways. Does every school have a creative cross-coverage model in place so that teachers tasked with other responsibilities are afforded time to help complete these tasks.

Treadwell Elementary School in Memphis is one example of a school that enacted a plan and implemented a creative model for coverage. Coverage was made available so that opportunities were given to teachers to carry out extra duties so planning and fair break times were protected for these teachers. There was also an intentional focus at the school on staff community building events. The staff recorded a 90 percent retention rate during the pandemic, a time when retention rates plummeted elsewhere. This simple, teacher-centered approach proved to be effective.[10]

This is the time and opportunity to create an extensive plan for one's school. Leaders should be looking at a comprehensive approach to physical and mental health for employees. Time, space, and opportunity for community building events to focus on that important sense of community should be prioritized. Is there a system for support to include mentoring and other support for educators? Do leaders reflect on this process so they are the ones who own it and if not, who will lead that change? Focusing on the teachers, who are the most crucial factor of student success, is where a renewed focus needs to be.

The next step is to add a teacher-centered layer into a school improvement plan and focus. Support for teachers' health and well-being is both actionable and measurable. The same statistics on attrition, respect, and satisfaction are ones that can be tracked and sought to be improved at any school or district. Actions such as scheduling regular, community building events, having a wellness plan for employees, increasing support for employees, and providing employees with the opportunities and resources they need can provide a positive impact leading to improvement in schools.

NOTES

1. Jake Bryant et al., "US K–12 Educators Are Thinking of Leaving Their Jobs | McKinsey," *Color Research & Application* 41, no. 2 (April 2016), 2.
2. Madeline Will, "Teacher Job Satisfaction Hits an All-Time Low," *Education Week*, April 14, 2022, sec. Teaching Profession.
3. Will, "Teacher Job Satisfaction Hits an All-Time Low."
4. "Present Company Included: Prioritizing Mental Health and Well-Being for All | McKinsey."
5. "Present Company Included: Prioritizing Mental Health and Well-Being for All | McKinsey."
6. Bryant et al., "US K–12 Educators Are Thinking of Leaving Their Jobs | McKinsey," 1–9.
7. CASEL, "What Is the CASEL Framework?"
8. Cynthia Cox Panchal,"The Landscape of School-Based Mental Health Services," KFF (blog).
9. "School Employee Wellness | Healthy Schools | CDC."
10. Bryant et al., "US K–12 Educators Are Thinking of Leaving Their Jobs | McKinsey," 11,12.

Chapter 10

Putting It All Together

Everyone wants to see all schools thriving. Professionals in education want success for all students. Society wants teaching to return as a noble profession that is respected and seen as a wise career choice. All involved want to do their best to realize these things. Currently schools are not as impactful or efficient as one wants and needs them to be. The answer to fixing this does not have to be starting over from the ground up. There are small yet powerful steps one can take right now to refocus time, energy, and resources on the way toward realizing the improvement and change that can be impactful. Now is the time to reflect while formulating and committing to a plan.

This text discussed the reality of differences that exist within educators. Adult learners have varied experiences that should be leveraged in learning design to help maximize the desired outcomes. Before one can leverage them, they need to accept, recognize, and understand them. Varied paths to education, whether a traditional or alternate route, affect what a teacher brings in their tool kit. Different colleges and the courses offered, chosen, and completed affect a teacher's personal skill set. Previous jobs in education, be it at different schools, districts, states, and countries all affect their unique strengths.

Varied skills and experiences are a benefit to the students they teach and interact with. Nobody wants a staff of identical robots. However, the challenge presented by these differences is the gaps in knowledge that exist because of this set of varied experiences. So, while one can recognize the benefits for their students, they need to equally recognize and accept the challenges it presents in a learning context. Keeping these differences at the forefront of one's thinking while designing any learning experience for staff as per the adult learner assumption, role of experience, is imperative. This requires differentiation.

However, the importance of a solution-oriented approach to moving forward is not just in recognizing these gaps in skills and knowledge. It lies in one's ability to forge a trusting and respectful climate. It lies in one's abilities to take the necessary time to really know all teachers, know their strengths, areas of improvement, and to make that a continuous process. Leaders are responsible for using needs assessments to maximize knowledge of coworkers and staff. This approach to data-informed action is necessary and should be expected for adult learners as it is for young learners.

This naturally transitions to the importance of adult learning theory in all one does regarding learning opportunities for teachers and staff. Knowledge of adult-learning theory was highlighted as a gap and potential barrier on the path to success. This text identified the lack of training and learning around adult-learning theory for both administrators and teacher leaders as a fixable problem, but one everyone must own before moving forward. The task of designing or facilitating learning experiences for adult learners is not being able to be effectively accomplished with an instructional approach from a pedagogy perspective.

Designers and facilitators of adult learning need tools and knowledge regarding andragogy to make learning experiences more impactful and successful. Beginning with the six assumptions of andragogy and a solid understanding of them for anyone charged with aspects of educating adult learners are necessary steps. The andragogical process model is a framework that designers of adult learning experiences should also receive adequate training on. Adult learning theory is a dense and evolving area of study and one that requires and deserves a larger place and priority in educational systems.

At both an immediate and micro level, one needs to provide training to all principals and teacher leaders who have any adult learning responsibilities. This is a pressing need and will impact the learning provided to teachers and staff. At a larger scale there needs to be revision to education programs. A highlighted focus should be placed on adult learning theory. Pedagogy is and should remain the primary focus during education programs in higher education. However, schools leverage teachers to design and facilitate learning experiences for adults, yet they are unprepared to do so. Higher education needs to adapt to support this reality.

In the meantime, colleges and universities can offer more opportunities on these topics to help meet the need and demand. This is possible because of the shrinking educational world. Continuing education, EdCamps, and MOOCs can be leveraged to grant leaders access to adult learning theory knowledge. EdCamps can be leveraged by local leaders to allow those with knowledge to share it with others. The ability to access learning through technology can further increase accessibility and expedite improving schools. This should not replace higher education's responsibility of revising college programs to build skills of teachers and building leaders.

With knowledge around how adults learn and how to best design learning experiences for them, one will see immediate improvement in practice and thus benefits to students. Approaching adult learners based on theory and best practice specific to how they learn will help to maximize outcomes and will shift how learners approach experiences. If learners' needs are met and designed for based on adult learning theory, the result will be experiences that learners are invested in. There will be a cultural shift in the way learning is received. This shift will allow improvement efforts to have a new realm of possibility regarding potential success.

Better knowledge about adult learning theory will improve design both for chosen and required training opportunities. Focusing on the assumptions of the need to know and readiness to learn, coupled with an understanding of self-concept will give the necessary attention to prework needed to get adult learners primed to receive the learning. There will always be some learning that needs to occur beyond a participant's choosing; one must use tools and knowledge to help it better meet the needs of adult learners. The more effective everyone is with this practice, the closer they can get to having effective systemic learning initiatives.

To have the most effective adult learning experiences, one needs the correct people in place at the most effective positions where they can affect positive change. A mindset shift in education to appreciate and leverage human resource development will help to achieve this. The focus should always be on maximizing assets. This occurs through building and improving skills, knowledge, and capacity. A focus in education should be on building skills, knowledge, and capacity in administrators, teachers, and staff, as well as transferring this to how they can positively affect their students and school community.

To develop human resources, one needs to have a clear vision about what they want them to accomplish. Refocusing or simply giving the ability for a principal to be a true instructional leader is a necessary step at schools that value that role. Allowing and empowering principals to use their time primarily being the instructional leader is this crucial step. This may necessitate delegating and sharing responsibilities with assistant principals and other staff members. An instructional leader needs the chance to be fully involved in all instructional aspects of a school to effectively identify and improve the educational functions.

The head of a company is afforded the all-important resource of time to do what is needed to make their company successful. A school needs to afford their leadership with the same opportunity. Time to be in classrooms, time to get to know their staff, and time to diagnose strengths and areas of improvement are all necessary functions of an instructional leader. They also need to have the opportunity to get to know their students. Time will be needed to become an expert on adult learning theory. Time will also be needed to apply this knowledge by designing learning experiences for their staff.

Keeping with human resource development, the idea of building capacity speaks to systemic initiatives. Having self-directed adults decide what they want to learn as their only growth opportunity will not have the impact necessary to help meet all their students' needs in the community they serve. Therefore, pairing best practices in adult learning theory within a transparent culture of learning and improvement can help to bridge what is important at a school or organization with what adults find relevance in learning. Balance between self-direction and systemic initiatives is crucial.

Taking a fresh look at what is important when evaluating teachers and leadership will help to change the culture of schools regarding improvement. Having teachers invested in systemic efforts needs to be an area of focus. Being part of larger-scale initiatives to better help students is a responsibility everyone should have and a necessary shift for systems to make to improve. So long as they provide educators with the support, resources, tools, and climate to grow for the betterment of students, this expectation is realistic and beneficial.

How one evaluates the position of an instructional leader in a school building is something that requires a shift. The typical administrative duties need to be shifted to other personnel so that instructional leaders have the time to realize their role. Being present in and leading the instructional aspects of their school, knowing their employees and students, and becoming an expert on adult learning theory should be where evaluation starts. Leading instructional rounds, co-teaching, providing support in practice and theory, including adult learning, are all responsibilities that should be focal points of the evaluation of an instructional leader.

Schools that get the systemic focus correct and have a textbook example of an instructional leader in place will be schools that can and will improve the human resource management functions of hiring and retaining excellent staff members. The idea of building capacity holds true on many layers and with many facets of a school. Satisfied and productive staff members will positively impact student learning. An active and skilled instructional leader will provide opportunities for learning experiences and support. All of this will lead to cultural shifts within the school that can impact every function of operations.

While the idea is not about rebuilding schools from the ground up, any change is difficult to successfully realize. This is why one must leverage any and all local resources they can. Change is a community effort. This requires engaged stakeholders. This involves leveraging as many resources as possible and it involves forging new relationships while further utilizing those already in place to help reach their goals. Resources are abundant, but it often takes reexamining relationships with local colleges and businesses to see what may be missing, what may need strengthening, or what can potentially become a new partnership.

Colleges and universities can gain mutual benefits from partnerships with local schools. Partnerships with local schools can yield valuable insight into current initiatives that schools are participating in, as well as issues they are facing. This two-way communication and relationship structure will allow professors and even students to support local schools while gaining data on topics that may need to be areas of focus in their school of education. Universities stepping away from theory and into practical application will benefit their staff and students alike while supporting local schools and their students.

Colleges and universities can create and offer continuing education credits to match initiatives that local schools are undertaking. Do not forget that through the shrinking educational world it does not have to be local colleges and universities, however, the benefits of local partnerships are many. Courses designed by those who have a background in adult learning theory are positive practices that benefit adult learners. This provides learning opportunities for teachers and staff, awareness of local higher education, and revenue for the college and university. It also offers opportunities for systemic learning to occur. This type of model is beneficial to all.

Beyond courses, statistical support is something that has long been needed in schools. This is not to say that schools are unable to use data. This is to highlight that if people with strong statistical backgrounds can help support schools with data analysis, everyone will be able to do more with the data they have and use it more appropriately and effectively. Schools have always had data to analyze. While data is a wonderful thing to have, it is only as good as the analysis that accompanies it and actions taken afterward. Everyone should be able to agree that the percentage of people in education with multiple college-level statistics courses is low.

Many decisions made in education regarding support, improvement initiatives, and resource allocations are based on data. Utilizing every available resource to help with this analysis should be a top priority for schools and districts. Any support from a local college or university would again provide a mutual benefit. Professors, statistics departments, and students could have current data to analyze. This type of authentic experience is valuable to all involved. Colleges and universities gain intimate knowledge of the types of assessments, and data points that are available as well, along with what they inform and the initiatives attached to them.

This author had the good fortune to attend a STEMposium a few years ago at a local university. The event included educational leaders from local schools, business leaders from local industries, and university professors. It was a magnificent event that pointed toward the importance of STEM (now often referred to STEAM to include art) in schools to help prepare young students for careers in related fields. There were speakers, demonstrations, audience questions, and participation. It was a wonderful opportunity to see what is happening in the local world pertaining to science, technology, engineering, and mathematics.

The biggest takeaway gained from this event occurred during a question-and-answer portion that focused on the local business leaders. The moderator asked the panel what the most important skill they look for and need in job candidates coming out of college. This referred to all candidates and all positions. There was a dramatic pause at the tables, and everyone in the audience mentally took guesses as to what that might be. Business leader after business leader, regardless of the sector, which included pharmaceuticals, medical, manufacturing, sales, engineering, technology, and many more all said the ability to analyze statistics and explain it to others was what they wanted and needed.

One leader elaborated to say, analyzing and conveying what statistics say is something a computer cannot do. They further explained that there is a continual need for someone to analyze and speak to statistics at board meetings, sales meetings, and development collaborations. While programs can do calculations, it is the people with statistical backgrounds and their knowledge of the data that makes all the difference in how they operate. This resonated back then and really resonates now when looking at areas where schools may be able to improve their approach to growth and improvement.

Being proactive and solution oriented should prompt immediate action in working closely with the local community and four-year colleges and universities to find ways to best leverage all opportunities that can benefit all stakeholders. Relationships already exist. However, it is time to reexamine how effectively and intentionally they are being used. School improvement efforts are supposed to be collaborative. Inviting one of the statistical supporters or someone from a local college to help at an improvement meeting should be the norm. There are always discussions at these types of meetings about how to support initiatives and teachers. Why not leverage academia?

Learning about statistics is also an area one can improve. Finding ways to incorporate learning opportunities for schools' instructional and teacher leaders are also worth exploring. The shrunken educational universe offers more opportunities to bring that type of learning to those who need it in education. Examining what is needed and making efforts to improve those areas is something everyone needs to be more proactive with. Realistically, statistical support from colleges and universities will be limited, so for those schools not fortunate enough to receive direct support, access to education is a great second option.

Beyond statistics one needs to broadly leverage the shrinking educational universe. The learning opportunities that exist for everyone online are too important not to make them a renewed focus of improvement efforts. The ability to participate in degree programs, continuing education credits, MOOCs, and EdCamps virtually opens the door to so many educational opportunities that were not available before. Communities and schools far from local universities have more equity and access than ever before. Find intentional and innovative ways to leverage new opportunities.

While degree programs are important, a focus here is on systemic improvement at a school or district level. School, instructional, and district leaders should be actively looking for opportunities to identify learning opportunities that can benefit their staff. Great learning opportunities are already created and exist that just need to be identified. Some of these are free of cost while others are not. Regardless, seeking out what exists is a key step in maximizing one's ability to provide meaningful learning opportunities to realize improvement.

Leveraging partnerships to have an online learning experience or course created is another option. Having learning take place online can shift the narrative from a singular learning event and provides access to learning at a time that is convenient to a learner. This will help meet assumptions of adult learners so readiness can be established, and the learner will have choices in when and where they complete their work. Systemic learning can still take place, but flexibility will help to meet adult learners' needs.

This is also the time to renew the challenge to states and districts to rethink licensure. Having licenses align to important skills and initiatives in education is a necessary area to explore. Instead of simply focusing on broad teaching categories, adding distinctions that mirror current areas of focus and research will help educators display their value. Forward thinking would be to attach assessments to this. The transparency that could be achieved through a process such as would benefit all stakeholders while placing a renewed focus on education and improvement

This text spent time addressing the importance of climate at a school. Climate goes well beyond the idea of physical space and its attributes; however, they are still important. One does not need a wing added to a school to better support the learning of its teachers. However, this text discussed repurposing a room to be the center of adult learning. If a school already has multiple teachers' lounges, an extra classroom, or a free corner of the library, any space will work. Making a commitment to prioritize the importance of a positive climate in a school sends a strong message to allow better learning to occur in a school.

The initial work can begin with physical space. Then the focus should shift to the color having a chance to positively affect learning. Next, one must ensure there is seating that promotes collaboration when desired. The availability for Wi-Fi access and ample power chords to charge and maintain charge of laptops also sets up the area to be a successful learning environment. Physical access to journals sets a tone for learning. Having visuals of a mission, vision and any instructional goals also helps to frame the area as one where learning occurs. These easy, cost-effective measures can positively affect the climate.

The most important aspects of climate for adult learners are having a trusting, respectful, and supportive environment. An instructional leader must prioritize this type of climate and culture for their staff. Without these key aspects, systemic learning initiatives cannot begin to meet the assumptions of adult learners. However, when the climate has shifted to become trusting, respectful, and supportive, adults can become ready for learning. Furthermore, an orientation for learning can be achieved with the right framing from the designer.

Now is also the time to focus on the teacher. Are teachers' needs being met? Is mental and physical health a priority for a school's adults? Are there improvement goals focused on mental and physical health and well-being of the adults who teach? Healthy teachers are present at school, and they will be more effective in instructing the students they are charged to serve. If this area is overlooked, now is the time to act. A goal and action plan focused on the wellness of the adults in a school is a way to help create a more complete community related focus to improvement. This is a simple yet powerful step forward.

All steps and concepts in this book are important and they are all to an extent connected. There is no perfect formula for how to improve schools. If one existed, everyone would be employing it. However, looking at the elements presented in this text can lead individual schools or districts toward a blueprint that can work for them. This book is really a call to reprioritize time and energy. It is a refocusing of good practices or missing practices. Sometimes the best answers for change and improvement are closer than anyone realizes.

Make time and effort to prioritize access to and learning around adult learning theory. This text just scratches the surface of the great work that is out there to support teaching and learning for adults. Make sure leaders understand the six assumptions of adult learners. Make sure that all who are working with leading adult learning learn more about the andragogical process model and how to lean on it as a guide to designing learning experience for adult learners. Then do not stop learning. As an instructional leader, teacher leader, district leader, find ways to grow and share that knowledge so adult learning is no longer in the background.

Do not stop there, shift the approach to a systems approach to learning. Develop the school's human resources for the good of the students they serve. Shift how one looks at successful performance and shift how they look at the instructional leader of a school. If that title is used, make sure it is what is being done on a day-to-day, minute-to-minute basis. Stay away from hollow verbiage and make sure everyone exemplifies the initiatives they undertake. An instructional leader must be fully invested in all instructional processes. The other parts of the job can and should be delegated both to others and in priority behind school improvement.

It is the instructional leader's responsibility to lead efforts to change the climate of a school. Make this a priority. Make space for learning to occur. Model how to best use that space and why it is important. Good leaders do not try to do everything on their own. Therefore, leverage local resources. Make new partnerships and strengthen existing ones. Seek help when help is needed and recognize when people have more expertise than one's staff possesses and find ways to let them help support the efforts of the school. School initiatives should be collaborative, so find ways for all stakeholders to contribute.

Finally, use the shrinking educational universe to one's advantage. The world has changed and continues to change the way education is accessed. This access should be something that leaders use to increase systemic and personal learning. Finding, designing, or having learning designed that will benefit school-wide or district-wide initiatives through online opportunities will help learning become and stay a continuous process for learners at schools. Learning is out there, getting it to those who need it is a small step that can make a significant impact.

Now is the time to act. Take a good look at a local school or district. Give an honest assessment of the most pressing areas where change needs to occur and prioritize that work. Commit to making changes and be proactive and intentional with decisions. Transparency with all stakeholders will help with realizing that vision and direction. Substantial change does not need to cost a lot. Leadership can affect change and should be the driver of that change. Best of luck and have patience. Change takes time and intentionality. These efforts will change how learning occurs and how improvement is realized.

Bibliography

Al-Ayash, Aseel, Robert T. Kane, Dianne Smith, and Paul Green-Armytage. "The Influence of Color on Student Emotion, Heart Rate, and Performance in Learning Environments." *Color Research & Application* 41, no. 2 (April 2016): 196–205. https://doi.org/10.1002/col.21949.

Bryant, Jake, Samvitha Ram, Doug Scott, and Claire Williams. "US K–12 Educators Are Thinking of Leaving Their Jobs | McKinsey." Www.mckinsey.com. Accessed March 2, 2023.https://www.mckinsey.com/industries/education/our-insights/k-12-teachers-are-quitting-what-would-make-them-stay.

CASEL. "What Is the CASEL Framework?" Accessed August 5, 2023. https://casel.org/fundamentals-of-sel/what-is-the-casel-framework/.

Glick, Margaret C. *Instructional Leader and the Brain: Using Neuroscience to Inform Practice*. Corwin, 2011.

Grissom, Jason, Anna Egalite, and Constance Lindsay. "HowPrincipals Affect Students and Schools a Systematic Synthesis of Two Decades ofResearch Commissioned By." Wallace Foundation, February 2021, https://www.wallacefoundation.org/knowledge-center/Documents/How-Principals-Affect-Students-and-Schools.pdf.

Hertz, Mary Beth. "Introduction to Edcamp: A New Conference Model Built on Collaboration." *Edutopia* (blog), September 29, 2010, https://www.edutopia.org/blog/about-edcamp-unconference-history.

Kapp, Alexander. *Platon's Erziehungslehre, Als Pädagogik Für Die Einzelnen Und Als Staatspädagogik*. Germany: Minden und Leipzig, 1833.

Knowles, Malcolm S., Elwood F. Holton, Richard A. Swanson, and Petra A. Robinson. *The AdultLearner: The Definitive Classic in Adult Education and Human Resource Development*. Ninth edition. New York: Routledge, 2020.

Magda, A. J., D. Capranos, and C. B. Aslanian. *Online College Students 2020: Comprehensive Data on Demands and Preferences*. Louisville, KY: Wiley Education Services, 2020.

Opper, Isaac M. "Teachers Matter: Understanding Teachers' Impact on Student Achievement." Rand.org. RAND Corporation. 2019, https://www.rand.org/pubs/research_reports/RR4312.html.

Panchal, Cynthia Cox, and Robin Rudowitz. "The Landscape of School-Based Mental Health Services." *KFF* (blog), September 6, 2022, https://www.kff.org/other/issue-brief/the-landscape-of-school-based-mental-health-services/.

"Present Company Included: Prioritizing Mental Health and Well-Being for All | McKinsey." www.mckinsey.com. Accessed October 10, 2022. https://www.mckinsey.com/mhi/our-insights/present-company-included-prioritizing-mental-health-and-well-being-for-all.

"School Employee Wellness." www.cdc.gov. Accessed September 16, 2020. https://www.cdc.gov/healthyschools/employee_wellness.htm.

Tomlinson, Carol Ann. *Differentiation of Instruction in the Elementary Grades. ERIC Digest.* https://eric.ed.gov/.

Wallis, Lynn. "Growth in Distance Learning Outpaces Total Enrollment Growth." State of Oregon Employment Department, March 4, 2006.

Will, Madeline. "Teacher Job Satisfaction Hits an All-Time Low." *Education Week*, April 14, 2022, sec. Teaching Profession. https://www.edweek.org/teaching-learning/teacher-job-satisfaction-hits-an-all-time-low/2022/04.

Wolfe, Pat. "The Role of Meaning and Emotion in Learning." *New Directions for Adult and Continuing Education*, no. 110 (2006): 35–41. https://doi.org/10.1002/ace.217.

About the Author

Dr. Kevin Popadines has spent over twenty years in education. He has held positions ranging from classroom teacher, school improvement chair, mentor, varsity basketball and golf coach to instructional specialist, professional learning specialist, acting administrator, as well as university-continuing-education course creator and instructor. Dr. Popadines has worked in public education for the states of New Jersey and North Carolina as well as for military-connected schools and currently works leading professional learning in Spain. He has a passion for learning and believes that a greater focus on adult learning theory, professional learning, and development of teachers can help yield increased achievement in schools.

www.ingramcontent.com/pod-product-compliance
Lightning Source LLC
Chambersburg PA
CBHW030147240426
43672CB00005B/302